DANGEROUS

PARENTING

DETOURS

DR. WALT BROCK

Iron Sharpeneth Iron Publications
A Ministry of Ironwood
Newberry Springs, California

THE IRONWOOD FAMILY TOOLBOOK SERIES

God's first institution, the family, is under attack more than ever! The Christian home is bombarded with immoral entertainment, deceitful philosophy, and humanistic education. The need for core, biblical values is the defense for such warfare. The Family Toolbook Series is designed to equip fathers, mothers, pastors, counselors, or teachers that serve families in the church or school setting by giving them practical guides to formulating a biblical foundation for life. This series covers fundamental truths that when applied become tools God can use to change lives.

Copyright 2003 by Walt Brock
ISBN 1-931787-08-5
LOC 2003116310

Unless otherwise noted, Scripture quotations are from the *King James Version*, and word definitions are from *Webster's 1828 Dictionary* or the *Strong's Concordance*.

Managing Editor, Shannon B. Steuerwald
Contributing Editor, Betty V. Brock
Cover and Layout Design, Susanna I. Capetz
Content Layout, Allison F. Pust

Iron Sharpeneth Iron Publications
A Ministry of Ironwood
Newberry Springs, California

FOREWORD

A number of years ago I was asked to conduct several sessions at a teacher in-service training week. In addition to the instructional sessions, the administrator asked me to teach a daily devotional on raising our children while serving in ministry. Betty and I were almost ending our child-rearing years and I had been mulling over the subject for some time. Over our twenty years of ministry, we had observed families where the children of Christian workers were not doing well —some situations were extremely heartbreaking. As we had gone away saddened by those circumstances, we wondered "why."

Over time, the Lord opened my eyes to these ten areas that are dangerous to the children of believers. They are dangerous because, at the time, they don't seem all that "big of a deal," yet the end results can be devastating. We had made diligent effort over the years to apply the principles to our own family, and the Lord was gracious in giving us the opportunity to see all four of our children accept the Lord as their Savior, graduate from Bible college, marry believers with a heart for God's work, and now serve the Lord in full-time ministry.

Since it is important that we understand the meanings of words as the Author (God, the Holy Spirit) meant, I have intentionally gone to the *Webster's 1828 Dictionary* for my definitions of words. A born-again believer, Noah Webster considered the Bible usage for each word in his dictionary as he settled on the correct definitions. The first dictionary written with American English as its basis and the closest chronologically to the King James Version of the Scriptures, this dictionary is in all likelihood the most accurate in its definitions of words used in the King James Version, which I have used exclusively.

My original title for these sessions that I've presented verbally many times was "The Devil's Decalogue of Dangerous Detours That Destroy the Destiny of the Descendents of Dedicated Disciples of Deity"—a mouthful! Later we published a few paragraphs of this "Decalogue of Detours" in ten consecutive issues of the *Ironwood Dispatch*. After receiving many requests for reprints and expansions, we decided to publish this book. While this process has taken much longer than I ever expected, I trust this book will encourage you to apply the Word of God to your home life and to find hope in God's promises. May God bless and strengthen your family.

In the Lord's work,

Walt Brock

CONTENTS

DETOUR 1.. 11
Delayed Discernment

DETOUR 2.. 29
Defiling Bitterness

DETOUR 3.. 45
Dishonorable Deportment

DETOUR 4.. 57
Disobeying Duties

DETOUR 5.. 81
Disbelieving Practices

DETOUR 6.. 93
Dominating Discontentment

DETOUR 7..113
Distracted Parents

DETOUR 8..123
Deliberate Despair

DETOUR 9..139
Deprived Discipline

DETOUR 10 153
Discouraging Dads

APPENDIX..173
Study Helps

ANSWER KEY..191

INTRODUCTION

Detours are universally despised. Yes, we may see some sights on a detour we would not have seen otherwise, but none of us shout for joy when we come upon a detour sign in our travels! Why? Well, detours almost always take longer, go over inferior roads, are poorly defined, and cost more since we must travel further to get to our destination. I have been on detours so long that some drivers actually turned around and headed back to their origin. Maybe they became confused and thought they were lost, maybe they questioned the wisdom of continuing on such a rough old road, maybe they wanted to explore a possible shortcut, or maybe they just got tired and quit. Whatever the reason—the time, the cost, the trouble, the confusion, the distractions—they stopped heading toward their destination. That's the kind of detours we are talking about in this book . . . detours that lead to nowhere but trouble.

The *1828 Webster's Dictionary* defines *detour* as "a turning, a circuitous way." *Circuitous* means "going round in a circuit" or "deviating from a direct line or course." Webster goes on to say that such indirectness in a moral sense means that someone is not "tending to a purpose by the shortest or plainest course"; thus acting in a "wrong or improper way." God has given us a very clear (not ambiguous) and direct (not winding) path to follow in our Christian living and in the rearing of our children. Leaving God's "straight and narrow" to travel on a detour leads to trouble, heartache, and chastisement from the Lord.

Detours are usually not dead ends. In reality sometimes they are, but they are not intended to be. They are alternate routes that lead back to the main road, notwithstanding all the wear and tear on our vehicle, pocketbook, energy, and nerves. Detours do not automatically determine that we will get lost or never get to our destination. This book identifies ten detour signs posted by parents, oftentimes not realizing they have put up their sign. Such signs can lead their children on a long and hurtful detour in life. The tragedy in all of this is that those signs were posted when the road, God's prescribed route, was a secure and safe one to travel.

Since God has given everyone a free will, parents' attitudes and actions do not automatically determine their children's attitudes and actions. However, if temptations come by the parents posting the detour signs directing away from God's way, children are highly susceptible to those temptations. As parents we need to look back down the road we have been traveling and see if we have been putting up, without realizing it, some detour signs for our precious little loved ones. Although there is no "determinism" involved here, no parent wants a child to travel unnecessarily down hurtful paths under the chastising hand of God. How much better would it be for us to be posting signs that say over and over, "This is the way; walk ye in it."

As you read this book, I suggest that you also look for unnecessary detour signs cluttering up the road of your life. Consider if a hazard from your past has been repaired but you neglected to take down the detour sign. Sometimes a discussion about those needed "life road" repairs you made in the past will help a teen or adult child choose to stay on God's direct route. The road of life the Lord has given us to travel needs constant work and maintenance (transformed and growing Christian) as well as correct signage (our testimony) to those who are following after us on the same road.

1

DETOUR

ONE

But strong meat belongeth to them that are of
full age, even those who by reason of use have their
senses exercised to discern both good and evil.
Hebrews 5:14

Delayed Discernment

*But strong meat belongeth to them that are of
full age, even those who by reason of use have their senses
exercised to discern both good and evil.*
Hebrews 5:14

Delay is costly. There is always a price to pay when deadlines
are missed. The IRS charges interest after April 15, credit card
companies add on late fees, and many a discount has been lost
because a coupon has expired. Procrastination is the "art" of putting things off until later, but it is almost always viewed negatively.
Everything from a gallon of milk to our driver's license has an
expiration date. One of the best ways to avoid difficulties in life
is to do everything in the proper time.

Older folks sometimes are viewed as being wise because they
have learned many of the lessons of life by experience. By listening to them we can often avoid making the same mistakes they
did. A smart person will learn from his own mistakes, but a wise
person will learn from the mistakes of others. We are told in
Ephesians 5:15-16 to live wisely by redeeming the time. Fulfilling
our responsibilities in a timely manner is wise living; developing
discernment, one of our most critical parental responsibilities,
must be timely in order to better teach and train our children.

Discernment can be defined as the ability to distinguish between
right and wrong or good and evil. To be discerning is to have the
wisdom to apply biblical precepts and principles to a variety of
situations and questions and then to be able to distinguish which
way or which answer would be more pleasing to God. Discern-

ment is the ability to see with the eye of faith God's viewpoint on any given issue.

The Scriptures teach that discernment is a learned skill. Proverbs was written to help us learn this wisdom and discretion (*Proverbs 1:2-4*), and *Hebrews 5:11-15* tells us that those who are able to understand the "strong meat" of the Word are spiritually mature (of full age) and trained to "discern both good and evil." If parents delay in learning biblical discernment, both they and their children will eventually pay the price.

We must remember that we are not talking about the discernment of our children. As important as it is for children to grow in this ability, the parents are the ones who need to have a well-developed discernment between right and wrong or between danger and safety. And they must be able to give a biblical explanation for their reasoning. *Proverbs 22:6* tells us, "Train up a child in the way he should go..." This verse clearly indicates that a child needs training and that parents are responsible for providing that training. Children lack wisdom and need help to develop it; if parents delay in developing the discernment they need to parent biblically, a dangerous detour lies ahead for their children. Parents can do nothing to guarantee that their children will, by their own free will, choose to do right; but if parents are themselves lacking in the spiritual wisdom to discern right from wrong, how will they ever hope to teach their children to make right choices?

"Everything means something." We use this saying at Ironwood as a constant teaching tool. The look on your face, the logo on your tee-shirt, the words you say, the music you like, the friends you have, the entertainment you enjoy, and the posters on your bedroom wall all mean something. If you're around young people very long, you will hear them say, "It doesn't mean anything" in order to rationalize an inappropriate behavior or form of entertainment. Settling the issue early in the conversation is always best. Everything does mean something! What part does discernment play in areas like these? Having discernment is not just saying that something is wrong or harmful, but it is giving a reasonable and biblical explanation of why it is wrong and what makes it harmful.

Discernment has two parts: the first half is recognizing that something may be evil or potentially dangerous, and the second half is teaching that recognition to our children and explaining our concerns about an issue. Saying, "because I said so," or "don't ask questions; just do what I say," or "because the preacher said so" are not enough. While these answers may be sufficient for very young children or in situations where we can't give a full explanation, eventually the child must understand why, or he will begin to doubt and then to reject our statements. Children who are consistently making wrong life choices lack real wisdom and have a need for a parent who will help them learn how to be discerning. Discipline alone will not produce long-term changes in children's decision-making. The scriptural model found in *Ephesians 6:4* is to "bring them up in the nurture and admonition of the Lord." Not only is the discipline (nurture) necessary, but also teaching (admonition), which is the application of the Scriptures to daily life. The result of failing both to discipline and to teach properly is to rear angry children who refuse to acknowledge that "everything means something."

When parents, who are responsible before God for the upbringing of their children, fail to develop within themselves a godly wisdom and discernment, the result is always the same. They cannot teach what they do not know, and the next dominoes to fall will be their children, who will, likewise, develop little or no discernment.

Parents fail to teach their children discernment for two reasons: they are either unable or unwilling to teach the "whys" of life to them. In exploring the first reason, we find a passage, *Hebrews 5:11-14*, which explains that some people who should now be teaching others are still in need themselves of learning the very simple and foundational truths of Scripture. They have not yet learned the wisdom that comes from a thorough study of God's Word. This passage refers to these people as "dull of hearing" or slow and sluggish to hear and learn. For one reason or another, these people have not learned to apply Scripture to their daily lives. They have not exercised their "senses...to discern both good and evil." The solution here is simple: reading, studying, meditating on, learning, and using the Scriptures for daily situations and decisions. Study aids are available and pastors can often give suggestions for good resource books. Acquiring these skills will take some time and effort; but knowledge and discernment, which are the natural fruit of such serious Bible study, will enable us to answer the "why" questions our teenagers bring to us.

Exploring the second reason of being unwilling is more challenging because it involves our basic motivations and life values. Remember the little saying, "everything means something"? What does saying "I am too busy" mean to a child? It means our priorities may be wrong, and to the child it means that whatever we are doing is more important than he is to us. Remember, children spell love: T-I-M-E. Would any Christian ever really believe that what he is "too busy" doing is more important than the eternal soul of his child? Everything means something. What does working so much our children never see us mean? What are we communicating if we don't take a stand on something the Scriptures clearly indicate is important? What are we saying when we don't make an effort to know what our children are thinking? What does saying "don't bother me now" mean . . . because it does mean something. What are we communicating when we ourselves can't discern between good and evil? I heard a statement some time back, "A successful parent is willing to do what an unsuccessful parent is not willing to do." Successful parents will be willing to put the necessary time and effort into developing spiritual discernment and then investing time in shepherding their children. Parents' learning to be discerning is an indispensable prerequisite to teaching discernment to their children.

How To Develop Discernment

Discernment basically means "to see or understand the difference, to be able to make a distinction between good and evil, truth and falsehood." *1 Thessalonians 5:21-22* gives us the complete process:

> Prove all things; hold fast that which is good. Abstain
> from all appearance of evil.

First, we are to "prove" or test "all things," a command to identify the differences between that which is good and that which is bad. Then we are commanded to make a decision that results in the action of "holding fast" to the good and "abstaining" from the evil. Three aspects are involved: evaluation, decision, and action. The key is the evaluation.

The problem we face in our society today is that as God has set forth the truth (His thesis) in the Word of God, the devil has introduced his ideas (anti-thesis) oftentimes easily identified as error. Then Satan holds out a culturally correct compromise (synthesis) and the temptation for us is to accept this as the new "truth for me" since it sounds like an acceptable compromise to our dilemma. We must never forget that any compromise with truth in fact compromises truth and makes it a lie disguised as truth. At the heart of spiritual discernment is the divinely-given ability to distinguish God's thoughts and ways from all others *(Psalm 119:66)*. As we are endeavoring to become discerning, we must remember that this is a process *(Proverbs 2:9-10)* that requires growth *(1 Peter 3:18)*. Once the evaluation has taken place, then we must have the willpower necessary to choose God's way and the faith to act in confidence knowing the decision is based upon God's revealed Word and will.

In making such evaluations, there are three basic steps to follow:
1. Answer prerequisite questions.
2. Follow spiritual discernment guidelines.
3. Formulate biblical principles to live by.

Step One—Answer Prerequisite Questions

1. Am I sure that I am saved?
2. Am I willing to go God's way if it is different from my way?
3. Am I now promising to prayerfully and honestly seek to understand God's Word with a goal of knowing God's way?
4. Do I really desire discernment in this particular area that I am questioning? Do I desire it enough to pay the price?

When one has honestly answered "yes" to all of these questions, he is ready to proceed to the next step.

Step Two—Follow Spiritual Discernment Guidelines

1. Pray consistently for wisdom and understanding concerning this area. *1 Kings 3:5-14; James 1:5*

   • Ask others to pray for you as Paul prayed for the Philippians.

Philippians 1:9-10—And this I pray, that your love may abound yet more and more in knowledge and *in* all judgment; That ye may approve things that are excellent; that ye may be sincere and without offense till the day of Christ.

- Pray consistently for God to open your understanding of the Scriptures and to use them to teach you to be wise and discerning.

  James 1:5-8—If any of you lack wisdom, let him ask of God, that giveth to all *men* liberally, and upbraideth not; and it shall be given him. But let him ask in faith, nothing wavering. For he that wavereth is like a wave of the sea driven with the wind and tossed. For let not that man think that he shall receive any thing of the Lord. A double minded man *is* unstable in all his ways.

- Ask God for wisdom because He will not "upbraid" or scold us for our current lack, if we are now seeking it.
- Ask God for wisdom because He answers this prayer "liberally," which means bountifully.
- Ask God for wisdom without "wavering" (doubting God) because He answers the prayer of faith.

2. Live in obedience now to that which you already know and understand from God's Word. God never shows us His will so we can decide later whether or not we will obey it.

   James 1:22—But be ye doers of the word, and not hearers only, deceiving your own selves.

3. Ask for advice from spiritually discerning church leaders and stay consistent in church participation. Pastors and church leaders are commanded to use the Scriptures in preaching and teaching to help believers grow in grace *(2 Peter 3:18)* for the perfecting (spiritual maturing) of the saints.

   Ephesians 4:11-14—And he gave some, apostles; and some, prophets; and some, evangelists; and some, pastors and teachers; for the perfecting of the saints, for the work of the ministry, for the edifying of the body of Christ: till we all come in the unity of the faith, and of the knowledge of the Son of God, unto a perfect man, unto the measure of the stature of the fullness of Christ: that we *henceforth* be no more children, tossed to and fro, and carried about with every wind of doctrine, by the sleight of men, *and* cunning craftiness, whereby they lie in wait to deceive.

4. Seek and pray for spiritual judgment from the Holy Spirit's illumination of Scriptures.

   1 Corinthians 2:11-14—For what man knoweth the things of a man, save the spirit of man which is in him? even so the things of God knoweth no man, but the Spirit of God. Now we have received, not the spirit of the world, but the Spirit which is of God; that we might know the things that are freely given to us of God. Which things also we speak, not in the words which man's wisdom teacheth, but which the Holy Ghost teacheth; comparing spiritual things with spiritual. But the natural man receiveth not the things of the Spirit of God: for they are foolishness unto him: neither can he know *them,* because they are spiritually discerned.

John 16:13— Howbeit when he, the Spirit of truth, is come, he will guide you into all truth: for he shall not speak of himself; but whatsoever he shall hear, that shall he speak: and he will show you things to come.

5. Study the Scriptures diligently. *Acts 20:28-32; Hebrews 4:12; 2 Timothy 2:15-16; 2 Timothy 3:15-17; Psalm 119:97-104*

    •   Look first for direct precepts and absolute commands from God regarding your area of concern.

    •   Develop principles for spiritual discernment from a study of the Word. Learning to think biblically through applying scriptural principles of the Word of God to our daily lives is where we find the real work of learning discernment. There are no shortcuts. (See the helps in the appendix.)

    •   Study consistently.

    •   Read a chapter of Proverbs every day corresponding to the day of the month. On the first day of a month read chapter one, on the second day read chapter two, and so on throughout the month. In months with just thirty days, you will need to double up one day. If you want to learn to think scripturally, do this every month for ten years.

    •   Study the Word in your daily devotions. See the helps for "Study of the Word" in the appendix.

6. Continue to grow. *1 Peter 2:2; Luke 2:52*

> *2 Peter 3:18*—But grow in grace, and *in* the knowledge of our Lord and Savior Jesus Christ. To him *be* glory both now and forever. Amen.

God uses different means to encourage and facilitate our spiritual growth. Our acceptance of His curriculum plans for our growth will affect whether we develop the discernment needed in the parenting process.

How Can I Grow?

By studying the Word in greater depth

> *1 Peter 2:2*—As newborn babes, desire the sincere milk of the word, that ye may grow thereby.

> *Hebrews 5:14*—But strong meat belongeth to them that are of full age, *even* those who by reason of use have their senses exercised to discern both good and evil.

By preparing your heart

> *Ezra 7:10*—For Ezra had prepared his heart to seek the law of the LORD, and to do it, and to teach in Israel statutes and judgments.

In *Matthew 13:18-23* we have Christ's explanation of the parable of the sower, which in its basic interpretation describes four different types of hearts and how those hearts react to the seed of the Word of God. The third type of heart, which is cluttered with materialism and the affairs of this life, most clearly describes the average Christian family today. The clutter in the heart causes us to be too busy in our lifestyle to have time to study the Word. "And the care of this world, and the deceitfulness of riches, choke the word" *(Matthew 13:22b)*.

By enduring the trials

> *James 1:2-4*—My brethren, count it all joy when ye fall
> into divers temptations; knowing *this,* that the trying
> of your faith worketh patience. But let patience have
> *her* perfect work, that ye may be perfect and entire,
> wanting nothing.

Many times trials or a crisis in our life motivates us to really dig
into the Word and grow.

By yielding to chastening

> *Hebrews 12:10-11*—For they verily for a few days
> chastened *us* after their own pleasure; but he for *our*
> profit, that *we* might be partakers of his holiness. Now
> no chastening for the present seemeth to be joyous,
> but grievous: nevertheless afterward it yieldeth the
> peaceable fruit of righteousness unto them which are
> exercised thereby.

God's chastening in our life will many times cause us to ask "why"
and thus be drawn to His Word and His way. The answer to our
"why" will always be the same: because He loves us.

By disciplining yourself

> *1 Timothy 4:7-8*—But refuse profane and old wives'
> fables, and exercise thyself rather unto godliness. For
> bodily exercise profiteth little: but godliness is profitable
> unto all things, having promise of the life that now is,
> and of that which is to come.

> *1 Corinthians 9:24-27*—Know ye not that they which run in a race run all, but one receiveth the prize? So run, that ye may obtain. And every man that striveth for the mastery is temperate in all things. Now they *do it* to obtain a corruptible crown; but we an incorruptible. I therefore so run, not as uncertainly; so fight I, not as one that beateth the air: but I keep under my body, and bring *it* into subjection: lest that by any means, when I have preached to others, I myself should be a castaway.

Developing biblical discernment is not for careless Christians. Without self-discipline discernment will not happen.

By aiming at biblical goals

> *Romans 8:29*— For whom he did foreknow, he also did predestinate *to be* conformed to the image of his Son, that he might be the firstborn among many brethren.

God's goal for us is to be conformed to the image of Christ (*1 Peter 2*). Remembering God's goal of Christlikeness and placing our goals of happiness, prosperity, or success secondary to His goal will change our perspective and help us to welcome His curriculum of growth.

Step Three—Formulate Biblical Principles to Live By

When the Scriptures do not speak directly, with an absolute command, concerning an issue before us today, we must develop and use biblical principles to apply to that issue. The Scriptures themselves give us an idea as to how to do this.

> *2 Timothy 3:16*—All Scripture *is* given by inspiration

of God, and *is* profitable for doctrine, for reproof, for correction, for instruction in righteousness:

Start with "the Truth," the Word of God. Find a passage or several passages of Scripture that speak to the area of your life you wish to address. Read the passage through. Study it out. Consider each step in the Bible formula below for change in your life. Record your thoughts and conclusions on the "Principles for Life" pages (reproducible page in appendix), one principle per page.

Doctrine

- What does it say? Study it out. Discern what the Bible actually says about this subject.
- What does it mean? Meditate (think about it) on what this passage means.

Reproof

- What do I need to repent of?
- Accept the reproof (shows you where you've been coming up short, sinning against God and man). The Holy Spirit convicts you of sin from this Scripture passage.

Correction

- What should I be willing to do? Respond to the correction (instructions on how to live obediently) of Scripture by submitting to it.
- Record the results on the "Principles for Life" pages. Write the principles you have learned from this passage of Scripture.
- Establish a goal to put this principle into your daily life. This has not been done if it is only in your head; it must be written out.

Instruction (Discipline) in Righteousness (Right Living)

- Begin the process of developing the discipline necessary to make daily decisions based on these principles. Over time daily decisions become godly habit patterns of living.
- Set up an accountability plan or journal, which is especially helpful in developing any new discipline.

Examples of Biblical Principles for "Doubtful" Activities

Listed below are some principles for proving (*1 Thessalonians 5:21-22*) or testing activities. When activities are neither specifically endorsed or condemned in the Bible, we may question whether we should participate or not. The question of our participation needs to be answered by the careful interpretation and honest application of such biblical principles, thus helping us to discern the wisdom of such participation by placing gray issues into either black or white columns.

1. Does it cause someone else to sin? Stumblingblock principle; the law of love—*Romans 14; 1 Corinthians 8; 1 Corinthians 10:23-33*
2. We are to lay aside sins and every weight that keeps us from being the best possible Christian. *Hebrews 12:1*
3. We are to make no provision for the flesh. *Romans 13:14; Galatians 5:16-22*
4. If it is doubtful, it is dirty. *Romans 14:23; James 4:17*
5. A Christian should be separate from the world. *2 Corinthians 6:14-7:1; Romans 12:2; 1 John 2:15-17*
6. Does it glorify God? *1 Corinthians 10:31*
7. Would Jesus Christ have done it? *1 Peter 2:21*
8. Would we be ashamed if Jesus Christ came and found us doing it? *1 John 2:28*

9. Can we feel free to do it when we remember that God, the Holy Spirit, dwells within us? *1 Corinthians 6:19*
10. Is it fitting conduct for a child of God? *Romans 2:24; Colossians 1:10*

Consequences of Continued Delay

What is the result of a parent's unwillingness to learn discernment and to teach it to his children? What does sending our children down this detour mean? It means that no beliefs and convictions will transfer from one generation to the next. It means that when our children are on their own, they will have no reason to choose what we have chosen. Will we have an answer "when thy son asketh thee in time to come, saying, What mean the testimonies, and the statutes, and the judgments, which the LORD, our God hath commanded you?" (*Deuteronomy 6:20*). Will we be prepared for the inevitable question, "Why?" We must not delay in developing biblical discernment and godly wisdom because that question will come, and will continue to come, until the child figures out that the parents have no answers. And then the silence will be deafening.

Companion Scripture Passages:
Hebrews 5:11-14
Deuteronomy 6
2 Timothy 1:3-9; 3:1-17
Proverbs 1-7

Discussion Questions:

1. What are the two parts of discernment?
   a. _____ evil.
   b. Able to _____ and _____ why.

2. Failure to adequately teach our children the "why" of an issue will cause them to first _____ and then _____ our statements and teaching.

3. What are the two reasons parents fail to teach their children discernment?
   a. They are _____.
   b. They are _____.

4. What is the first prerequisite to developing discernment?

5. List 6 guidelines for developing discernment.
   1.

   2.

   3.

   4.

   5.

   6.

6. What does the saying, "everything means something" mean to you?

7. What is the reason that beliefs and convictions are not transferred from one generation to the next (my children)?

2

DETOUR

And ye have forgotten the exhortation which speaketh unto you as unto children, My son, despise not thou the chastening of the Lord, nor faint when thou art rebuked of him.
Hebrews 12:15

DEFILING BITTERNESS

*And ye have forgotten the exhortation which speaketh unto you
as unto children, My son, despise not thou the chastening of
the Lord, nor faint when thou art rebuked of him.*
Hebrews 12:15

Bitterness that comes from not forgiving someone for violating
our rights, taking advantage of us, or hurting us in some way
can be absolutely disastrous to our children. Such bitterness
really is the result of unresolved anger, sometimes directed toward a particular individual or organization and sometimes so
unfocused that we aim at anyone coming across our path. The
problem is not that we sometimes become angry, but that the
anger is unresolved, has been nurtured, and has grown into bitterness. Then we speak and act out of that bitterness and defile
our children, sending them down a dangerous detour. As harmful as an unforgiving spirit is in the heart of a child, parents do
the real damage when they refuse to forgive and have growing
within themselves a spirit of bitterness, which will in turn defile
those around them.

The Scriptures clearly teach that bitterness is a root sin which
hurts many people, most often and most harshly those who are
the closest to the embittered person. *Hebrews 12:15* says,

> Looking diligently lest any man fail of the grace of God;
> lest any root of bitterness springing up trouble you, and
> thereby many be defiled.

Since the result of bitterness is the defiling of others, under-standing the word *defiled* helps us to comprehend the nature and seriousness of this detour. As we read the *Webster's 1828 Dictionary* definition of *defile,* place your child's name as the object of the defilement.

1. To make unclean; to render foul or dirty; in a general sense.
2. To make impure; to render turbid; as, the water or liquor is defiled.
3. To soil or sully; to tarnish; as reputation.
4. To pollute; to make ceremonially unclean.
5. To corrupt chastity; to debauch; to violate; to tarnish the purity of character by lewdness.
6. To taint, in a moral sense; to corrupt; to vitiate; to render impure with sin.

From these definitions, we can see that the defilement that bitterness causes can truly harm our children. How can we protect them against such a miserable future?

Protecting Our Family

Protecting ourselves and our children from bitterness, while challenging, is far from impossible. God has given us ways to keep bitterness from creeping into our lives. He has also pro-vided in His Word clear instructions for eliminating bitterness if it has already gained an entrance. Some decisions must be made right at the start if we desire to absolutely stay off this detour.

We need to take special care not to exhibit, in any way, an un-forgiving, bitter spirit before our children. We must control our attitudes and actions and especially our conversation, bridling our tongues as we would restrain a horse using a bridle *(Psalm*

39:1). But primarily we must guard our heart, "for out of it are the issues of life" *(Proverbs 4:23).*

We must also understand that we usually direct our bitterness first toward authority: God, parents, employers, teachers, church leadership, civil authority, etc. Next in line is our own family: grandparents, children, siblings, or extended family members. From there, we can focus our bitterness on friends, co-workers, neighbors, church members, and people in widening circles until we despise anyone who crosses us in any way.

Some people who truly do not realize they are bitter are, in fact, not bitter toward other people, but toward God. They blame God for their problems or a loss they have suffered. They blame God for either causing the hurt or failing to stop the hurt from happening. Sometimes they must deal with their own past, such as parents failing them, abuse at the hands of others, or a physical handicap. Bitterness directed at God, for whatever reason, comes from a combination of a self-focus and a failure to understand God, His nature, and His love.

Because this process grows slowly in hidden areas, we need to recognize some warning signs of this deadly sin. Among others, they include the following:

- Self-pity, especially its enjoyment
- Persistent, negative thoughts about others
- Focus on our violated "rights"
- Critical words (*Ephesians 4:29*)
- Third-party involvement—telling others how we've been wronged in order to draw them to our side
- Thoughts of retaliation—"I'll get mine" or "I'll get even"
- Desire to avoid "offenders"—leaving the room when they walk in

- Sarcastic remarks
- Constant feelings of being treated unfairly
- Diminishing sense of gratitude to God for both the good things in our life and bad things (*1 Thessalonians 5:16-18*)
- Holding of grudges (*Ephesians 4:26*)
- Inability to see the good or positive side of people
- Feelings that everyone is out to get us

If bitterness, for whatever reason, has crept into our lives, defilement of those around us, including our children, is not far behind. The first step in protecting our family is to recognize that bitterness is a sin and confess it to God as such. Then in a humble spirit, we must ask Him for His grace to help us deal with this progressively difficult sin.

> *1 Peter 5:5a-6b*—For God resisteth the proud, and giveth grace to the humble. Humble yourselves therefore under the mighty hand of God.

Once we have taken these general steps in the right direction, there are three specific ways we can protect our family. First, we can protect our family through preempting bitterness, not ever letting it get a toehold in our lives. Second, we can protect our children through reconciliation, solving the bitterness through forgiveness. Finally, we can work to protect our family through a self-sacrificial others-first love.

Protection Through Preemption

Of the three ways to deal with this problem, the best approach is to keep bitterness from even beginning to grow by controlling through God's grace and help our reactions to the circumstances and people God has allowed in our life. *Colossians 3:12-14* is one of several passages of Scripture that will give us a handle on how God wants us, through His power and grace, to face such difficult situations of life.

> Put on therefore, as the elect of God, holy and beloved, bowels of mercies, kindness, humbleness of mind, meekness, longsuffering; Forbearing one another, and forgiving one another, if any man have a quarrel against any: even as Christ forgave you, so also *do* ye. And above all these things *put on* charity, which is the bond of perfectness.

This passage includes seven heart responses which, by grace, we can cultivate and thereby forestall the defilement of bitterness. Each of the seven responses is also supported by a description of true biblical love found in *1 Corinthians 13*, the love chapter.

Cultivate Mercy

Definition:
- Compassion, pity, tenderheartedness
- Bowels were considered the seat of tender affections and emotions
- The ability to look at the other side of the story
- Being sympathetic to one another

Exercising a spirit of mercy involves seeing every situation from the other person's viewpoint. It is no mistake that this is first, because by doing so we will often eliminate the need for any further action on our part.

1 Corinthians 13:5—seeketh not her own.

Cultivate Kindness

Definition:

- Kind feelings and good thoughts put into words and action
- Benevolence one to another

Kind thoughts of compassion are not enough; kind words and actions.

1 Corinthians 13:4——is kind.

Cultivate Humility

Definition:

- Modesty, sense of one's littleness
- Having a humble opinion of oneself
- Gentle ways
- Not a self-view; but an others-view

Humility is a byproduct of our realizing the goodness and greatness of God. It is not cultivated by thinking lowly of ourselves, but rather by not thinking of ourselves, but others.

1 Corinthians 13:4——charity vaunteth not itself, is not puffed up.

Cultivate Meekness

Definition:

- A temperate spirit that accepts all of God's dealings with us as good
- Without disputing or resisting; not angry with God or others
- Submissive to God's Word
- Being willing to be governed or under authority——*James 1:21*

- Considerate when confronting others—*Galatians 6:1-2; 2 Timothy 2:25; 1 Corinthians 4:21*

A spirit of meekness helps us to understand that God often uses hard situations in our life to help us grow. This takes a real faith to believe that God is good, that He loves us, that He knows all about our situation, and that He has allowed it to happen. Can we thank God for that?

1 Corinthians 13:5-6—vaunteth not itself, is not puffed up.

Cultivate Longsuffering

Definition:
- Patience when ill treated or provoked by others
- No anger or thoughts of revenge

Reacting with patience is hard to do, but is essential if we are to eliminate bitterness before it starts *(James 1:2-4).*

1 Corinthians 13:4—charity suffereth long, is not easily provoked.

Cultivate Forbearance

Definition:
- To bear with, to endure
- Our response to the unintentional faults or carelessness of others, even when no effort to improve is evident

Forbearing one another—this is turning the "patience" up one notch and requires even more of God's grace to help us forbear with another's weaknesses.

1 Corinthians 13:7—beareth all things.

Cultivate Forgiveness

Definition:

- To show one's self as gracious, kind, and benevolent
- To grant forgiveness; to pardon
- Not absolution from all consequences, but relationship restoration is the result

We now go past longsuffering and forbearance; we have been willfully wronged. The Bible instructs us to forgive one another, be willing to forgive, or have the spirit of forgiveness.

1 Corinthians 13:8—never faileth; *13:7*—hopeth all things, endureth all things.

Protection Through Reconciliation

The second approach to avoiding this defiling detour is to resolve difficulties as they arise in a biblical way. If we don't, bitterness will definitely spread to those around us (*Proverbs 22:24-25*). The biblical formula is to obey *Luke 17:3-4* and *Matthew 18:15-17*:

> *Luke 17:3-4*—Take heed to yourselves: If thy brother trespass against thee, rebuke him; and if he repent, forgive him. And if he trespass against thee seven times in a day, and seven times in a day turn again to thee, saying, I repent; thou shalt forgive him.

> *Matthew 18:15-17*—Moreover if thy brother shall trespass against thee, go and tell him his fault between thee and him alone: if he shall hear thee, thou hast gained thy brother. But if he will not hear thee, then take with thee one or two more, that in the mouth of two or three witnesses every word may be established. And if he shall neglect to hear them, tell it unto the church: but if he

neglect to hear the church, let him be unto thee as a heathen man and a publican.

If we have a true cause of offense, our responsibility is to go to our Christian brother and confront him or her in a "spirit of meekness" (*Galatians 6:1*); if he will not talk to us or address the issue, then we must follow *Matthew 18* and take a spiritually mature person with us who is impartial enough to listen to both sides of the story and tell us that we are wrong, if necessary. (If both parties to the conflict are in the same church, it is best to keep the resolution process within the confines of the local church using the church's leadership.) If he repents, then it is now our turn to forgive him in the same way Christ has forgiven us—totally.

When we stand at the judgment seat of Christ, how many of our sins will Jesus have forgiven? Obviously, the answer is "all of them," for even one unforgiven sin would send us to hell for eternity. In the same way, we must forgive others fully and freely. When can we stop forgiving someone for a repented sin against us? We can stop whenever we want Christ to stop forgiving us of our repented sin against Him! In other words, we can never stop being willing to forgive. How do we know if others are sincere in asking for forgiveness? We don't! Some positive indicators might be an attempt at reconciliation and restitution or a focus on the problems that their offense has created for us, but, whether they are sincere or not, if we have honestly forgiven them, we have destroyed the power of bitterness in our life.

Protection Through Love

The last way to deal with the problem of defiling bitterness is the least desirable and potentially the most difficult. If we have allowed bitterness to fester in our heart and have not been successful in sincerely and humbly seeking reconciliation, we must work on this problem alone, relying on the promise that Paul writes in *Philippians 4:13* where he says, "I can do all things through Christ which strengtheneth me." This is an enormous challenge which requires an understanding of and obedience to Christ's command recorded in *Matthew 5:4*. Jesus says, "But I say unto you, Love your enemies, bless them that curse you, do good to them that hate you, and pray for them which despitefully use you, and persecute you." We can glean four simple principles from this command that we can follow in order to keep our children from the detour of defiling bitterness.

Principle Number One—Right Attitude

Jesus says, "Love your enemies." We must have a forgiving attitude toward even those who are called our enemies. The word *enemy* carries the idea of hostility or adversary. We can apply this word to anyone with whom we are having a conflict and who will not cooperate with our attempts at reconciliation. So, we do what Christ commands, we love them! Is loving this way hard? Actually, it is impossible without the Lord's help. Should we wait until the other has repented or reformed? Christ does not wait for us to respond to Him. Paul says in *Romans 5:8* that Christ loved us *before* we were a Christian, and He continues to love us. We should not wait either. Love is a self-sacrificing willingness to put someone else's interests ahead of our own concerns (*Ephesians 5:2*). We must genuinely have this love for those who've hurt us because our attitudes are read and copied by our children; we cannot fake "a sweet spirit" for long. Those who know us best, our family, will recognize and learn what we really think. Who said the Christian life was easy? No way!

Principle Number Two—Right Words

Jesus says, "Bless them that curse you." First, a right attitude...and now right words. Notice that while others are saying bad things about us, we must be saying good things about them; no payback, getting even, or returning in kind what they've said about us. We can teach our children no greater lesson than, by our example, showing them how Jesus would react to hurtful words. We must be aware of and careful about how we talk about others, especially when our children can overhear our conversations. Critical, unforgiving, and unkind words about others will corrupt our children. Often people say the right words, but with a tone and body language that says loudly and clearly, "I'll not forgive." Such thinly, disguised attempts are easily interpreted by children. Astonishingly, parents sometimes talk to their children, trying to get their children on their side or to use them as a "sounding board," filling them in on all the sinful details. Such words only cripple our children's ability to form future, long-lasting relationships.

The other danger is that, long after we have settled this problem, our children, who took up our offense, will suffer from the bitterness which has spread its roots into their lives, and thus the defilement has passed to the next generation. On the other hand, if we restrain our tongue from evil but instead "speak blessing," we will edify and "minister grace" to them (*Ephesians 4:29*).

Two areas of greatest challenge are when family members have been offended by other family members or when parents in church leadership have been criticized by other church members. When those we love or those we serve hurt us, kind words are often far from our thoughts. Christ is our example of responding in a loving manner to all those who insulted Him with their words. If our "at home" reaction to such insults (whether true, deserved, or not) is not Christlike, we will be posting another detour sign for our loved ones.

Principle Number Three—Right Action

Jesus says, "Do good to them that hate you." Words are important, but they should be supported by action. Doing something nice for someone we like or who probably will return the favor is easy. To have a forgiving attitude, which produces acts of kindness for an enemy, requires an exercise of grace. *Webster's 1828 Dictionary* defines *grace* as "the free unmerited love and favor of God, the spring and source of all the benefits men receive from Him." God's grace gives us salvation, and His grace working through us strengthens us to "do good to them that hate you." If we want to obey this principle, we cannot entertain even the thought of revenge or of getting even. We must instead "overcome evil with good," obeying Paul's instruction in *Romans 12:19-21*, "Dearly beloved, avenge not yourselves, but rather give place unto wrath: for it is written, Vengeance is mine; I will repay, saith the Lord. Therefore if thine enemy hunger, feed him; if he thirst, give him drink: for in so doing thou shalt heap coals of fire on his head. Be not overcome of evil, but overcome evil with good."

Principle Number Four—Right Prayers

Jesus says, "Pray for them." Offended folks may ask, "What if I don't feel like praying for my enemies?" This question is a good indicator that we have progressed to the "bitterness" stage, for bitterness defiles our relationship with Jesus Christ Himself. It is so important to relay to our children this fourth principle in order to combat the defiling detour of bitterness. Praying during a family prayer time for

God's blessing on our enemies communicates a forgiving attitude to our children and will help us, by God's grace, to have the biblical attitude of love and forgiveness which will produce Spirit-filled actions. If we are honestly having trouble responding biblically, we must pray and ask God to give us the grace to obey His Word through faith. Laying our burden in the hands of the Lord is the final step in handling unresolved problems. When we pray for our enemies, we will experience a peace that only God can give us even in the midst of trials and tribulations. We won't have to work at obeying the command to be thankful in all things; we'll just be thankful.

The right attitude revealed through right words, right actions, and right prayers will do wonders in keeping our children away from the detour of defiling bitterness that could literally de-rail them for life!

Companion Scripture Passages:
Matthew 18:15-35; Luke 17:3-4—forgiveness of others
Hebrews 12:1-15—example of Christ
Romans 8:31-39—love of God
Genesis 37; 39-41; 50:15-21—life of Joseph

Discussion Questions:

1. How could having a parent who harbors bitterness in his heart toward others hurt a child?

2. Love is a _____willingness to put others ahead of ourselves.

3. Blessing (saying good about) others is evidenced through right _____, then right _____ and deeds.

4. Cursing (saying bad about) others is evidenced through wrong _____, then wrong _____ and deeds.

5. Bitterness directed toward God Himself comes from an _____of God and a _____-focus mentality.

6. Discuss ways we can protect ourselves by cultivating right attitudes and thus prevent slipping into the sin of bitterness.

7. Do we need to go back and mend attitudes that our children may now have because of something we've said about friends, family, or leadership?

3

THREE

Honor thy father and mother; which is the first
commandment with promise; that it may be well with
thee, and thou mayest live long on the earth.
Ephesians 6:2-3

DISHONORABLE DEPORTMENT

*Honor thy father and mother; which is the first
commandment with promise; that it may be well with thee,
and thou mayest live long on the earth.*
Ephesians 6:2-3

This is a dead-end detour! Of all the detours we are looking at, this one has the potential of being the most disastrous to our children. On the other hand, avoiding it will produce one of the greatest blessings parents could possibly desire, the promise of God for both length and quality of the life for their children.

God first gave man His Word in written form when He wrote the Ten Commandments and gave them to Moses on Mt. Sinai. Since they were the first words literally written by God to man, we should consider them carefully. The first four commands focus on man's relationship to God, while the last six precepts concern inter-personal relationships with other people. God's order is always important, and the first one of the six commands dealing with man's relationship to man requires children to honor their parents. I would submit to you that its primary place on the list of relational commands means that we should consider it a foundational principle, underlying all of our relationships in life. As the apostle Paul indicates in Ephesians, God considered honoring parents important enough to make it the first command with an attached promise.

> *Exodus 20:12*—Honour thy father and thy mother: that
> thy days may be long upon the land which the LORD

thy God giveth thee.

Ephesians 6:2-3—Honour thy father and mother; (which
is the first commandment with promise;) that it may
be well with thee, and thou mayest live long on the
earth.

The verb *honor* means to show respect for someone. Its Hebrew
root means to "make heavy," which came from the practice of
assigning value to something by adding more volume and thus
adding to the weight of the precious metal being paid for an item.
So we can define *honor as a decision to add to the weight or value
of a person*, thereby placing greater worth on someone and then
showing that value through one's actions, words, or attitudes.
God addresses this command to children, but parents bear some
of the responsibility for whether or not their children respect
them. Since the quantity and quality of our children's lives are so
vital, it is absolutely essential that they learn to obey and respect
(honor) their parents. Young children cannot understand the
concept of honor, but they reveal that attitude by the way they
obey. God established this connection between honor and obedience, which explains why *Ephesians 6:1* says "obey" and *Ephesians
6:2* says "honor"—one leads to the other just as surely as the
elementary years lead to those of junior high, unless, of course,
parents complicate the situation by dishonorable deportment
of their own. The key question parents must answer is, "Do our
lives encourage our children's respect or disrespect?" The future
happiness of our children depends on our honest answer.

Additionally, the book of Proverbs points out the importance of
the parents' example in reaching their children's hearts. *Proverbs
23:26* says, "My son, give me thine heart, and let thine eyes
observe my ways." So what kind of "ways" are we talking about?
We all have some ideas and opinions on that question, but let's

examine a few verses of Scripture concerning this subject. We should point out here that we are not suggesting sinless living. That would be impossible and to pretend to be "sinless or fault-less" before our children will actually lead to disrespect. As in most situations, our reactions are more important than our actions. In other words, forgetting we promised to do something with one of our children disappoints them, but denying having made the promise or passing it off as no big deal multiplies the problem. Such reactions can badly detour them into despising us and then reaping all the negative results God has promised would follow such an attitude.

Dishonorable Deportment from Proverbs

It is quite easy to generalize the principles of how parents should encourage the respect of their children; however, facing the specific application of such principles with actual do's and don'ts from Scripture is where "the chickens come home to roost." In Proverbs, we can find several such practical applications, both positive and negative, that address parental deportment and the results in regards to honor and respect.

1. **Displaying Pride**—a spirit of "know-it-all-ism"

   Proverbs 15:33— The fear of the LORD *is* the instruction of wisdom; and before honor *is* humility.

   This parent can never admit he is wrong, ask for forgiveness, listen to advice, or think that his children's opinions are worthy of consideration. There is no need to seek an opinion outside of himself. He knows it all.

2. **Diluting Lukewarmness**—little or no evidence of a real reverential fear of God, He believes he can do it all without God's help

Proverbs 22:4—By humility and the fear of the LORD are riches, and honour, and life.

Remember what *Revelation 3:15-20* says about God's attitude toward the lukewarm believer. My experience of over thirty years of ministry largely aimed at reaching young people for the Lord has convinced me that reaching children from truly spiritual families or from clearly Bible-rejecting homes is much easier than ministering to young people from "worldly friendly" Christian families (*James 4:4*). Why? In any family with parents who live consistently, the children respect (honor) their parents. Lukewarm parents are major potholes in children's lives because of the disrespect their deportment generates.

3. **Inconsistent Decisions**—in such concerns as rules, actions, reactions, and reasons, there is little consistency or follow through

   Proverbs 25:19—Confidence in an unfaithful man in time of trouble is like a broken tooth, and a foot out of joint.

   How do you think children respond when they are asked, "What habit/characteristic about your parents makes you angry?" Their number one answer is inconsistency. Changing rules, showing favorites, not following through, setting unclear/uncertain punishments, and a whole host of such inconsistencies really anger children. Everything can't be nor should always be equal, but things should always be just. I have heard parents say, "If you want to see inconsistency, just look at my kid! He has no room to talk." Now, that may be true, but our child is still in the process of growing to maturity, and we are supposed to be already mature, or at least mature enough not to be measuring our behavior by his. He should be following and learning from our example.

4. **Ongoing Disagreements and Strife**—having an argumentative spirit of strife as the common mode of communication in the home, or using loud shouting and arguing as a tactic to get our way

   Proverbs 20:3—It is an honour for a man to cease from strife: but every fool will be meddling.

   If we take a concordance and find the word *strife* in the Bible, we will only have to look up thirty-nine verses, but if arguing has become a way of life in our home the context of those verses ought to scare us to death. The word *strife* means engaging in selfish self-promotion in a quarrelsome and argumentative way. The entertainment media repeatedly portrays families in America as argumentative and verbally aggressive; our children are surrounded by this behavior which is rooted in self-love rather than an others-first love. Our Christian homes should display a marked difference that fosters mutual respect for one another.

5. **Deceitful Hypocritical Behavior**—saying and doing one thing at church or in the presence of certain people and behaving an opposite way at other times

   Proverbs 20:7—The just man walketh in his integrity: his children are blessed after him.

   2 Corinthians 8:21—Providing for honest things, not only in the sight of the Lord, but also in the sight of men.

Most parents would be surprised at how quickly children recognize this behavior. Maybe parents even brag in their presence about how they "really put one over on that guy." Deception usually starts out small; for example, having our children tell someone on the phone that we're not home when we really are, inventing excuses for our children's missing homework, or calling in to work "sick" when we really just want a day off. But these deceptions easily grow into more serious lies, and eventually our lives completely lack integrity.

If a parent practices these five negative behaviors, the child will more than likely dishonor his parents, as well as be provoked to anger *(Ephesians 6:4)*.

Honorable Deportment from Proverbs

After looking at the negative aspects of our example and how easy it is to undermine our children's respect for us, it is refreshing to turn our attention to three positive practical applications that Proverbs gives us to help our children fulfill their biblical mandate to honor Mom and Dad. A warning however, being positive does not make them any less difficult to follow through with.

1. **Diligent Detection**—searching out the truth of a matter, especially in relation to reports from school or church leadership regarding the behavior of our children
    Proverbs 25:2b—But the honor of kings is to search out a matter.

    Never mind their protestations about privacy. Our children will only respect us if we keep digging until we get to the real and total truth of the matter. If we let them "put one over on us," they will go away more convinced than ever about how to get things done in this world and with a dwindling supply of honor for Mom and Dad. Remember the cardinal rule for raising children—all children are born sinners, and *all* means all! When our children are very young, we should require full disclosure of what is under the bed, in drawers, on the radio, in the CD collection, on the bookshelf, etc. If we wait until we have a problem, we've probably waited too long. When can we trust our children? A discerning study of *Luke 16:10-11* will answer that question. Trust can only be built by being trustworthy.

2. **Development of Wisdom**—learning to bring up our children wisely

    Proverbs 4:7-8—Wisdom is the principal thing; therefore get wisdom: and with all thy getting get understanding. Exalt her, and she shall promote thee: she shall bring thee to honour, when thou dost embrace her.

    We must beg God for wisdom; we must search diligently for it *(James 1:5-6)*. We can become much wiser than we are right now simply by reading one chapter of Proverbs every day of the month and by applying these principles to our life. Again, children do not need to see perfection, but they ought to see some evidence of growth. *Wellsprings of Life* by Donald Orthner is a good resource in applying Proverbs and the material in chapter one of this book will be helpful in developing wisdom.

3. **Encouragement of Respect**—accomplished by consistent living and purposeful teaching

    Proverbs 26:1—As snow in summer, and as rain in harvest, so honour is not seemly [fitting] for a fool.

Proverbs 26:8—As he bindeth a stone in a sling, so is he that giveth honour to a fool.

Children honoring their parents is foundational for their future and their prospect of joy in this life. While children are commanded to honor their parents and will be individually held accountable for their behavior in that area, we as parents bear part of the burden by being honorable parents. Such character and behavior will encourage our children's respect and thus acquire for them the foundation for all their future relationships, namely the ability to "honor all men." As shown in the verses above, honoring those who are not honorable (foolish) is incongruous; such honor does not make sense and is extremely difficult to give. What a disadvantage and tragedy it would be for our children to go through life without learning to honor and respect others.

Do we love our children's future enough to change our current behavior, practices, and lifestyle so as to encourage their honor of us? I hope so, because without that encouragement our children will face the great temptation of turning off onto this dead-end detour. Have you ever noticed that dead-ends always end before you get there? Without God's promise of blessing for long life, our children run the risk of their life ending in a dead-end before they "get there."

Companion Scripture Passages:

Exodus 20:1-17—Ten Commandments

Ephesians 6:1-4—Key passage on parent responsibility

Revelation 3:15-20—What God thinks about lukewarm Christians

Proverbs 1:8-9; 2:1-20—Result of teaching biblical wisdom by a respected parent.

James 3—A look at offenses and a life lacking in integrity, and wisdom's effect upon that life

Discussion Questions:

1. What are the five negative things that parents can do that will result in the children being tempted to dishonor the parents?

   a. _____ pride.

   b. _____ Christians.

   c. _____ decisions.

   d. _____ and strife.

   e. _____ behavior.

2. What are the two positive suggestions for helping our children respect us?

   a. Diligent _____ work.

   b. Developing and learning biblical _____.

3. How can these two parental practices result in children respecting their parents?

4. Why do we believe that respect is the foundation for relationships in life?

5. Never admitting they have been wrong or have failed in some way is an evidence of a parent _____ _____. Why?

6. Can you think of examples from your past where those over you disappointed you by their lack of consistency or proper example? If yes, how did that affect you? Were there any long-range consequences that still have not been completely dealt with? If so, see chapter two.

4

DETOUR

FOUR

*But I would have you know, that the head of
every man is Christ; and the head of the woman
is the man; and the head of Christ is God.*
1 Corinthians 11:3

DISOBEYING DUTIES

But I would have you know, that the head of
every man is Christ; and the head of the woman
is the man; and the head of Christ is God.
1 Corinthians 11:3

In the last three chapters, we have been discussing the ways that the devil is attacking our families by tempting each family member to follow a detour from God's prescribed way. Even if detours seem sensible when we are in the middle of dealing with a situation, they are still detours. We must remember that Satan is a deceiver and a liar from the beginning, and, because he has had several thousand years to practice his craft, he is getting better at deception all the time. Our only hope is to hold tenaciously to the Scripture and to do all we can to follow God's Word in our lives *(Colossians 2:7-8).*

Authority is the core issue in this detour and violating God's principles concerning authority is to set the stage for children to be rebellious. *Webster's 1828 Dictionary* defines *authority* as "1. Legal power, or a right to command, or 2. The power derived from opinion, respect or esteem; influence of character or office."

In the family we have both kinds of authority: the given and the earned. As parents, we must exercise the authority God has given us over our children and live our lives in such a way that we earn our children's willing and respectful obedience. There are a number of ways we can, without realizing it, shove our children down this dangerous detour of disobedience resulting in destruction.

The two most common ways relate to the husband-wife relation-ship of the parents: first, when the husband does not fulfill his God-given role as the loving leader of the home; and second, when the wife rejects her God-given responsibility to lovingly submit to the headship of her husband.

Accountability Factor

Husbands and wives need to live together in the family in Christ likeness. A husband is commanded to be the head of the home and to love his wife as Christ loved the church, giving himself to his family as Christ gave Himself for the church (*Ephesians 5*). Headship is the role God has given to men in a marriage union between two people who are spiritually equal. The husband has the awesome responsibility of leading the union in a way that will please and glorify God. God holds husbands accountable for their leadership, or their lack thereof, in the home.

A wife is commanded to submit to her husband "as to the Lord" or "as is fitting in the Lord" (*Ephesians 5:22; Colossians 3:18*). This submission is a voluntary yielding in love "to another who is equal in importance and essence."[1] It is an "inner quality of gentleness that affirms the leadership"[2] of the husband. God holds wives accountable for their submission or their lack thereof in the home.

The fact that a husband has been busy with work and is tired when he gets home is not a reason for him to give up the leadership of his family. The fact that her husband is slow to make decisions or reluctant to exert spiritual leadership is not a reason for the wife to usurp his responsibility and authority. Any time we reject our God-given roles in the family, we are teaching our children to do the same with their own roles. Children, especially teenagers, are very perceptive about these matters. They are quick to discern that something is not right, even when Mom and Dad think they are doing "O.K." or believe that living more "culturally-sensitive" than biblically obedient is "O.K. in these modern days." They may be unaware that they are undermining God's blueprint, but the teens will be sensitive to the departure *(Proverbs 14:12)*.

Sowing and Reaping Factor

Not only will God hold parents accountable, but danger lies ahead for anyone who forgets the sowing and reaping principle as it relates to family roles. Paul writes in *Galatians 6:7-9*:

> Be not deceived; God is not mocked: for whatsoever a man soweth, that shall he also reap. For he that soweth to his flesh shall of the flesh reap corruption; but he that soweth to the Spirit shall of the Spirit reap life everlasting. And let us not be weary in well-doing: for in due season we shall reap, if we faint not.

Husbands who reject or ignore their responsibility to lead their family are sowing the seed for unruly children, and wives who refuse to submit to their husbands in the Lord are sowing the seed for rebellious children *(Titus 1:6; 1 Timothy 3:3-4)*. Refusal to obey God's commands and principles concerning the respective family roles of husband and father or wife and mother will reap a harvest of rebellion in children. If our children are rebellious, we might ask our pastor or a trusted counselor to help us look honestly for rebellion in our own life first. We seldom recognize this disobedience in ourselves, but I am convinced this detour is first being modeled by husbands and wives and then being imitated by children. That's a shame, because our families are the ones that have the most to lose if our children stay on this destructive detour.

The way parents handle their God-ordained roles of husband and wife will reap corresponding fruit in their children. The effect is unavoidable, even if Mom and Dad's attitudes and actions are not overtly rebellious. The children, especially as they move into puberty and beyond, will absorb and respond to what is really going on, even if they don't realize they are doing so, producing either a blessing or a curse. The harvest depends on what "seed" has been sown. Remember, the law of the harvest teaches that one always reaps the same as one has sown, reaps later than the sowing, and reaps more than was sown. So in the case of our children, the family roles we play will be multiplied and may not be manifested until years later as our children become teenagers and young adults. We are not proposing a type of "determinism" where parents absolutely control the future of their children, but Scripture certainly teaches that parents have a greater influence on children than anyone else and strongly point them in the direction of their course in life.

Because of our inescapable influence as parents, we must be diligent in sowing the proper biblical truth and example in our children's lives. Because this influence is so profound, we must be very clear on and committed to God's teaching on family roles.

God's Image
Let's begin at the beginning with the creation account recorded in *Genesis 1:27*, "So God created man in his own image, in the image of God created he him; male and female created he them." Though we must believe it, we may never completely understand, until we get to Glory, how we have been created in God's image. Perhaps one of those ways would be in His triune nature:

three distinct parts (Father, Son, and Spirit), equal in essence and worth, yet different in function. In the same way, when God tells us that a husband and wife are "one flesh," we must believe it: two distinct beings, equal in essence and worth, become one. This truth concerning one flesh could not have a stronger place in Scripture, recorded in the Old Testament, in the Gospels as Christ's words, and as doctrine in the Epistles. We may not understand this fact of oneness, but we must believe it.

> *Genesis 2:24*—Therefore shall a man leave his father and his mother, and shall cleave unto his wife: and they shall be **one flesh**.

> *Matthew 19:5-6*—And said, For this cause shall a man leave father and mother, and shall cleave to his wife: and they **twain** shall be **one flesh**. Wherefore they are no more **twain**, but **one flesh**. What therefore God hath joined together, let not man put asunder.

> *Mark 10:8*—And they twain shall be one flesh: so then they are no more **twain**, but **one flesh**.

> *Ephesians 5:31*—For this cause shall a man leave his father and mother, and shall be **joined** unto his wife, and they two shall be **one flesh**.

God's Value System

The Scriptures says that God values men and women equally:

• Both man and woman bear God's image equally.

> *Genesis 1:27*— So God created man in his **own** image, in the image of God created he him; male and female created he them.

- We are all one in Christ.

  Galatians 3:28— There is neither Jew nor Greek, there is neither bond nor free, there is neither male nor female: for ye are all **one** in Christ Jesus.

- Husbands and wives are both heirs together of the grace of life.

  1 Peter 3:7— Likewise, ye husbands, dwell with them according to knowledge, giving honor unto the wife, as unto the weaker vessel, and as being **heirs together** of the grace of life; that your prayers be not hindered.

God's Organization

We derive the organizational chart (see Appendix) from *1 Corinthians 11:3,* "But I would have you know, that the head of every man is Christ; and the head of the woman is the man; and the head of Christ is God." If we will study it, we will see the lessons that God wants us to understand and obey ourselves and then teach to our children. This passage teaches that God is in control, not man. Men and women often concentrate on the "submission/headship" issues as they relate to each other, but the real issue relates to our obedience to God. In following her husband, the wife is obeying the Lord; likewise, in lovingly leading the home, the husband is obeying the Lord.

1 Corinthians 11:3 is not the only reference in Scripture which teaches levels of function. Just a quick consideration of the Scriptures locates three other contexts in which a hierarchy functions according to God's will. The order of creation, the results of the fall, and the relationship of Christ to the church all teach the necessity of differing functions and an hierarchy of organization to carry out those functions properly.

The Order of Creation Teaches Us God's Organization for the Family

First, let us consider the revelations in *Genesis 2:18-25:*

> And the LORD God said, It is not good that the man should be alone; I will make him an help meet for him. And out of the ground the LORD God formed every beast of the field, and every fowl of the air; and brought them unto Adam to see what he would call them: and whatsoever Adam called every living creature, that was the name thereof. And Adam gave names to all cattle, and to the fowl of the air, and to every beast of the field; but for Adam there was not found an help meet for him. And the LORD God caused a deep sleep to fall upon Adam, and he slept: and he took one of his ribs, and closed up the flesh instead thereof; and the rib, which the LORD God had taken from man, made he a woman, and brought her unto the man. And Adam said, This is now bone of my bones, and flesh of my flesh: she shall be called Woman, because she was taken out of Man. Therefore shall a man leave his father and his mother, and shall cleave unto his wife: and they shall be one flesh. And they were both naked, the man and his wife, and were not ashamed.

God created man first, and then He created the woman to be a "help meet," a suitable helper for her husband. God said that being alone was not good because He created us as relational beings. He desires that we enjoy a strong and close fellowship with Him, an intimate relationship with our spouse, and a love and unity with all believers. Only in certain situations has God called and given grace to those he wishes to remain single so that they can devote all their attentions to their relationship with

Him, to their fellowship with other believers, and to the work of the ministry (*1 Corinthians 7*).

When God surveyed His finished creation of the first family, He declared it to be "good," and then right from the beginning, He gave some guiding principles for this new family.

First, He said they were **to "leave" father and mother.** Newly married couples need to leave the parent's home and establish a separate home and family. The order seems backwards and illogical, but the instructions are clear; and we must obey in faith, or we will be doing this job of "family" without God's blessing.

Second, Adam and Eve were not only to leave, but also **to "cleave,"** which means to "join fast together, to glue, to cement." This word indicates a very strong union. I do a little woodwork in my garage and have, on a number on occasions, glued two pieces of wood together. I have found where the joint was a good one, that the glued joint was stronger than the wood itself. The wood actually broke before the glue joint gave away. I have also found in every case that the wood is literally stronger as two pieces of wood glued together than it would have been as one piece. God never intended the husband/wife union to dissolve, and as a couple "bonded," they are actually stronger than each would be separately. The whole is greater that the sum of its parts.

Third, the **"one flesh" principle** is not speaking only of the physical union (a key component), but includes soul-oneness. It is the essence of complete intimacy as these two become one.

The **absence of shame** is the fourth principle and indicates that there should be a genuine deep intimacy that is physical, emotional, and mental. The reality of this intimacy is established out of the other three principles; for each of them are required in order to form the kind of real sharing relationship, which would produce such freedom in being one with the other without shame.

The Results of the Fall Teach Us God's Organization for the Family

After the fall, as God talks with Adam and Eve, He explains the functions of husbands and wives in a cursed world. What had been natural and good before the fall, now had to be commanded and became very hard to do.

> *Genesis 3:16-20*—Unto the woman he said, I will greatly multiply thy sorrow and thy conception; in sorrow thou shalt bring forth children; and thy desire shall be to thy husband, and he shall rule over thee. And unto Adam he said, Because thou hast hearkened unto the voice of thy wife, and hast eaten of the tree, of which I commanded thee, saying, Thou shalt not eat of it: cursed is the ground for thy sake; in sorrow shalt thou eat of it all the days of thy life; thorns also and thistles shall it bring forth to thee; and thou shalt eat of the herb of the field; in the sweat of thy face shalt thou eat bread, till thou return unto the ground; for out of it wast thou taken: for dust thou art, and unto dust shalt thou return. And Adam called his wife's name Eve; because she was the mother of all living.

This passage not only establishes differing roles in the home, but it very clearly indicates who the responsible leader of the family is to be. From this time on, God has held and will hold men accountable for how they have lead and influenced their families either for righteousness or for the worthlessness of "mammon" (*Matthew 6:19-20,24*). Godly husbands and fathers will receive the rewards reserved for those who have obeyed God's plan for the family; men who have failed in their responsibilities before

God will suffer painful loss at the judgment seat of Christ. Likewise, God told Eve, standing for all wives, that Adam would "rule" over her (*Genesis 3:16*). In the *Theological Word Dictionary of the Old Testament, Volume 1*, the word *rule* means "to exercise dominion,"[3] and by using it, God is very clear about His requirements that a husband lead his family and that a wife follow that leadership. If either one rebels against God's commands in this area, either passively or aggressively, the family will harvest the spoiled fruit of the disobedience, and may continue to do so for generations to come.

The Relationship of Christ to the Church Teaches Us God's Organization for the Family

The third, most important, and clearest instruction from the Scripture on God's plan for husbands and wives in marriage is found in *Ephesians 5:22-33,* which clearly depicts the relationship between husbands and wives as a type of Christ's relationship with His bride, the church.

> Wives submit yourselves unto your own husbands, as unto the Lord. For the husband is the head of the wife, even as Christ is the head of the church: and he is the savior of the body. Therefore as the church is subject unto Christ, so let the wives be to their own husbands in every thing. Husbands, love your wives, even as Christ also loved the church, and gave himself for it; that he might sanctify and cleanse it with the washing of water by the word, that he might present it to himself a glorious church, not having spot, or wrinkle, or any such thing; but that it should be holy and without blemish. So ought men to love their wives as their own bodies. He that loveth his wife loveth himself. For no man ever yet hateth his own flesh; but nourisheth and cherisheth it, even as the Lord the church: for we are members of his

body, of his flesh, and of his bones. For this cause shall a man leave his father and mother, and shall be joined unto his wife and they two shall be one flesh. This is a great mystery: but I speak concerning Christ and the church. Nevertheless let every one of you in particular so love his wife even as himself; and the wife see that she reverence her husband.

The Wife's Role

This passage begins by admonishing wives to submit to their own husbands, meaning that wives should voluntarily obey God's directions for family roles and organization. As the wife submits herself to "her own husband," she teaches her children by example how they should submit to God in salvation and as believing members of the church. What an awesome responsibility mothers have. To follow, voluntarily, the leadership of her husband, even though this submission may be hard, is by example teaching her children how to respond to God's commands even when they don't like them or don't understand them. Obedience is never tested when we are asked to do something we want to do anyway, but rather, when we are told to do what we do not wish to do. God never commands the husband to force his wife to submit; her yielding is to be voluntary, as is our relationship to Christ. The husband is commanded to love her and lead her in such a way that she will want to follow him. Men, it is hard enough as it is for our wives to obey this command by faith; let's not compound the issue by being "jerks" and failing to lead in a God-honoring way. If we love our wives as Christ loves the church, their submission to our leadership will more likely follow. Just as with husbands, wives may look forward to the judgement seat of Christ for a reward for their voluntary submission in love, thus living an object lesson before their children.

Submission Qualifiers

Submission does not mean wives give up thinking for themselves, are stupid, are incompetent, should be fearful or timid, or should put their husband in the place of Christ in their own lives. There are several biblical "qualifiers" concerning their submission.

- **The spiritual qualifier**, "as unto the Lord," indicates to submit except when submission would be sin.

- **The moral qualifier** of *Titus 2:5* says the wife should be obedient, yet chaste, which means free from moral defects. Therefore, she should not submit to an immoral directive.

- **The influence qualifier** of *1 Peter 3:1-7* says the wife should influence her husband for righteousness. Submission does not mean that the wife should just turn off her brain and go mindlessly after a husband leading in the wrong direction. She is to be a help suitable for her husband who needs her cautions, ideas, and input on situations; God has established ways and means for a wife to influence her "own husband." There is a delicate balance here, for a wife could easily use this influence as an excuse for not submitting to her husband. Sometimes a wife may think, or even know, her husband is making an unwise decision, but she must submit to her husband by faith in God, believing His way is best (*Proverbs 14:12*). If God's Word will be violated by her obedience, she needs to obey God first, of course; but if there is no clear violation of God's Word, she must honor and follow her husband—no matter how foolish his decision may seem. Submission is an attitude which produces actions; and children will be taught rebellion by a wife who does outwardly what her husband wants, but inwardly entertains a disrespectful heart attitude. Her unbiblical influence is that of an unsubmitted heart.

The Husband's Role

The major emphasis of this Ephesians passage, however, is on the husband's role as the loving leader in the home. Since "the husband is the head of the wife," he has the responsibility to lead her. What does *the head of* mean? The same word is used in *1 Corinthians 11:3*. *Vine*'s says that it is used "metaphorically, of the authority or direction of God in relation to Christ, of Christ in relation to believing men, of the husband in relation to the wife, of Christ in relation to the Church, Ephesians 1:22; 4:15; 5:23...."[4]

Much debate has gone on in circles that study leadership on what is the difference between the two concepts, leadership and management. Leadership has to do with direction, vision, and purpose. It includes influencing people to work diligently to accomplish the purpose. It also includes establishing values and the basic policies within which the manager is to accomplish (plan, organize, lead, and control) the vision and purpose initiated by the leader. Both aspects have some of the other in them and both are a function of the husband in the Christian home if he is going to be a biblical husband.

Leadership Qualifiers

Man exercises his authority as a delegated authority from God. Man will be held accountable for not only his headship, but also for *how* he exercises that headship. There are a number of biblical relationship guidelines that give direction to a man's leadership of the home, which come primarily from the example of Christ's relationship to the church.

- **A self-sacrificing relationship**—Because of His love, while we were yet sinners (*Romans 5:8*), He gave Himself for us.

71

Ephesians 5:2—And walk in love, as Christ also hath loved us, and hath given himself for us an offering and a sacrifice to God for a sweet-smelling savour.

Ephesians 5:25—Husbands, love your wives, even as Christ also loved the church, and gave himself for it.

- **A listening relationship**—He is always available to talk "seeing he ever liveth to make intercession for them" (*Hebrews 7:25*). He not only listens, but also He feels with us and knows our needs.

Hebrews 4:15-16—For we have not an high priest which cannot be touched with the feeling of our infirmities; but was in all points tempted like as we are, yet without sin. Let us therefore come boldly unto the throne of grace, that we may obtain mercy, and find grace to help in time of need.

- **A mutual, helping relationship**—As the wife is the helpmeet to her husband, so Christ relies upon us to spread the gospel and do the work of the ministry.
Romans 12:1—I beseech you therefore, brethren, by the mercies of God, that ye present your bodies a living sacrifice, holy, acceptable unto God, which is your reasonable service.

Ephesians 5:1-2— Be ye therefore followers of God as dear children: And walk in love, as Christ also hath loved us, and hath given himself for us an offering and a sacrifice to God for a sweetsmelling savor.

- **A providing relationship**—As Christ provides for the saints, so a husband provides for his family.

Philippians 4:19—But my God shall supply all your need according to his riches in glory by Christ Jesus.

- **A cherishing relationship**—Cherish means to keep warm, to heat. The idea is to care for as a nursing mother would care for her child. It is the opposite of neglect.

  Ephesians 5:29—For no man ever yet hateth his own flesh; but nourisheth and cherisheth it, even as the Lord the church.

- **A nourishing relationship**—Nourish comes from a root word that refers to feeding. Implied here is the meeting of someone's fundamental needs for food, shelter, communication, etc.

- **An exclusive relationship**—Jesus wants no object, goal, or person to come between Him and us. Compare *Ephesians 5:30-32* with the following verses.

  James 4:4-5—Ye adulterers and adulteresses, know ye not that the friendship of the world is enmity with God? Whosoever therefore will be a friend of the world is the enemy of God. Do ye think that the scripture saith in vain, The spirit that dwelleth in us lusteth to envy?

- **A purifying relationship**—Jesus' goal is to present His church pure and holy, without blemish, at the judgment seat of Christ. Likewise, the husband's goal should be to teach, mentor, and help his wife to become spiritually mature and complete.

Ephesians 5:26—That he might sanctify and cleanse it with the washing of water by the word, that he might present it to himself a glorious church, not having spot, or wrinkle, or any such thing; but that it should be holy and without blemish. So ought men to love their wives as their own bodies. He that loveth his wife loveth himself.

- **A knowledgeable relationship**—Christ knows all about us (*Hebrews 4:12-16*), therefore husbands should seek to know as much about their wives as possible.

Hebrews 4:12-16— For the word of God *is* quick, and powerful, and sharper than any two-edged sword, piercing even to the dividing asunder of soul and spirit, and of the joints and marrow, and *is* a discerner of the thoughts and intents of the heart. Neither is there any creature that is not manifest in his sight: but all things *are* naked and opened unto the eyes of him with whom we have to do. Seeing then that we have a great high priest, that is passed into the heavens, Jesus the Son of God, let us hold fast *our* profession. For we have not a high priest which cannot be touched with the feeling of our infirmities; but was in all points tempted like as *we are, yet* without sin. Let us therefore come boldly unto the throne of grace, that we may obtain mercy, and find grace to help in time of need.

1 Peter 3:7—Likewise, ye husbands, dwell with *them* according to knowledge, giving honor unto the wife, as unto the weaker vessel, and as being heirs together of the grace of life; that your prayers be not hindered.

- **An honoring relationship**—Christ has "crowned" man with "glory and honor" (*Psalm 8:5*), creating him a free, moral agent and dying for each person individually. His standard of honor is evidenced by his communication and provision. Likewise, husbands need to respect and honor their wives, evidenced through their willingness to communicate by listening and understanding.

  Ephesians 5:33—Nevertheless let every one of you in particular so love his wife even as himself; and the wife *see* that she reverence *her* husband.

  1 Peter 3:7—Likewise, ye husbands, dwell with *them* according to knowledge, giving honor unto the wife, as unto the weaker vessel, and as being heirs together of the grace of life; that your prayers be not hindered.

Looking at all of these together, we can recognize that husbands need to be loving leaders. The chart, "Loving Leadership" (see Appendix) will help outline the scriptural characteristics of a loving leader.

The Biblical Concept of Ruling in Relationships

Another concept that we must understand is translated "rule" in *1 Timothy 3:4-5, 13,* as Paul instructs Timothy about what God requires of church leaders. God never has a double standard and what He requires of those in leadership, He desires for all men. *The Theological Dictionary of the New Testament* defines *rule* (Greek word *proistemi*) as "to put before, to present," or, in the intransitive middle, "to go before, to preside," and figuratively "to surpass, to lead, to direct, to assist, to protect, to represent, to care for, to sponsor, to arrange, to apply oneself to."[5] The two meanings usually entailed are "to lead" and "to care for," and in *1 Timothy 3:4-5*, ruling and caring are closely related. The point in *1 Timothy 3:12* is similar: deacons should be heads of their households, but with an emphasis on taking proper care of them. The combination of leading and caring that one may see in the New Testament usage agrees well with the principle of *Luke 22:26* that the leader is to be a servant. Putting these two words in today's terminology, we would say that ruling is very close to managing. Louis Allen, in his book *The Management Profession*, divides management into four types of work:[6]

1. The work of **planning** includes such things as planning for the future, setting goals, coming up with programs and schedules, setting up a household budget, and establishing the family's rules, policies, and traditions.

2. The work of **organizing** includes figuring out how to do something, dividing up the work load in the home (delegation), and establishing how people are to relate to one another and function together.

3. The work of **leading** includes the crucial skill of decision making: gathering all the necessary information, making a list of pros and cons, figuring out what the alternatives are, and choosing from the list of alternatives. Good decision making is a skill that can be learned. Leading also includes giving direction in a positive way so that those under us will be motivated to follow without coercion. Using and modeling proper communication is also necessary to successful leadership. As fathers we must learn to listen and listen well to our entire family, because we are an example to our children of how Jesus Christ listens to us when we pray. Helping those under us to grow and develop is another aspect of leadership.

4. The work of **controlling** includes the process of using good judgment to determine where our children are in their development, knowing what they need most, and figuring out ways to measure their progress. There is a saying in management circles that goes like this, "What gets measured gets done." I have seen the truth of that statement over and over. Evaluating our goals for our children, measuring their progress, and developing a way to make corrections are all involved in this aspect.

The Positive Attitude in Relationships

Colossians 3:19 provides us one final qualifier, "Husbands, love your wives, and be not bitter against them. To avoid bitterness, husbands must control their own spirits, by God's grace. *Vine's Dictionary* says that *bitter* comes from a root word that means to prick or cut.[7] If husbands are to avoid becoming bitter against their wives, they must not become irritated or exasperated or harsh in attitudes, words, or actions toward their wives or their own children. Some who violate this principle actually exhibit more patience and self-control with others than with their own wives. As husbands lovingly lead in the home, they are responsible before God to control themselves and to treat their wives as they would want Jesus Christ to treat them.

Conclusion

If wives do not submit to their husbands and honor them, if husbands do not love their wives and lead them, they will push their children down the detour of rebellion and disobedience to God. What kind of harvest will we have? The seed we are sowing now will determine what and how much we will harvest in the future.

[1]Piper, John, and Gruden, Wayne. *Recovering Biblical Manhood and Womanhood.* Wheaton, Illinois: Crossway Books, 1991, page 196.

[2]Ibid., page 196.

[3]Kittel, Gerhard, and Friedrich, Gerhard, Editors. *The Theological Dictionary of the New Testament, Abridged in One Volume.* Grand Rapids, Michigan: William B. Eerdman's Publishing Company, 1985, page 534.

[4]Vine, W. E. *Vine's Expository Dictionary of Old and New Testament Words.* Old Tappan, New Jersey: Fleming H. Revell Company, 1981, page 202

[5]Kittel, page 534.

[6]Allen, Louis A. *The Management Profession.* New York: McGraw-Hill, page 68.

[7]Vine, page 129.

Companion Passages:
Ephesians 5:22-33; Colossians 3:17-19; 1 Corinthians 11:3— Husband and wife relationships

Galatians 6:7-9— Sowing and reaping

1 Peter 3:1-7— Responsibility for mutual influence within a marriage union

1 Corinthians 7:2-5— Defraud ye not one another

Discussion and Study Questions:

1. What are the two kinds of authority in the family?
    a. _____ authority
    b. _____ authority

2. What are the two most common ways we can detour our children onto the detour of rebelliousness?
    a. Through the father's failure to _____ _____ _____the home
    b. Through the mother's failure to biblically submit to the _____ of her husband

3. Submission is the _____ yielding in love to another who is _____ in important.

4. Headship is the _____ God has given men in marriage between two spiritually _____ people. The husband is also commanded to _____ his wife self-sacrificially.

5. How can we be sure we are not leading our children into the destructive detour of rebellion by unwittingly violating God's established order for the family?

6. How can a husband, using unbiblical domination, as head of the home frustrate his wife and anger his children?

7. How can a wife, with good intentions, usurp her husband's authority or manipulate around it? What effect will this have on the children?

8. Who is in control in the home? _____

5

DETOUR

FIVE

Let no man despise thy youth; but be thou an
example of the believers, in word, in conversation,
in charity, in spirit, in faith, in purity.
1 Timothy 4:12

DISBELIEVING PRACTICES

*Let no man despise thy youth; but be thou an
example of the believers, in word, in conversation,
in charity, in spirit, in faith, in purity.*
1 Timothy 4:12

The power of accumulation is an amazing thing! Perhaps you've played that children's game of trying to get someone to give you a penny a day for a month and persuading them to double it everyday for the next month. It is surprising to see that a penny doubled every day quickly multiplies to well over a million dollars before the end of the month.

The Power of Example

The accumulation principle propels the power of example. This principle does not in any way diminish the importance of single acts and the lasting impressions they can leave upon our children; however, the enduring, determining force behind the power of example comes from the accumulation of little things over time. These subtle accumulations over time can profoundly affect a life and mold a character.

What are we teaching our children through the little things we do or don't do each day of our lives? Do we pray for wisdom and help concerning daily decisions? Is giving both to God and to others a way of life for us? How have we been showing our love for God through serving in our church? Are our spiritual gifts well used or unused? What do our entertainment and music choices communicate? Do we talk about the Lord in front of our children? Do they see us studying the Bible at home, or do we pick it up only as we are leaving for church? Do our decisions and commitments reveal that a desire for money and things is our real goal in life?

Some examples of inconsistency might help us to understand what we are talking about.

- A parent can say "amen" when the preacher says we all need to read the Bible daily, but at home, his children know that he never reads the Bible himself.
- A child gets a spanking for lying, yet Dad isn't truthful to the neighbors, or he makes promises he never intends to keep.
- Parents pretend at church that everything is going fine at home, but they argue and bicker or don't talk to each other the rest of the week.
- Parents never pray about decisions.
- Parents make choices only on the basis of money.
- Parents take credit for all the good things and blame others or God for the bad things that happen in their lives.
- Mom submits to her husband on the surface, but manipulates him every chance she gets.
- Dad requires the children to obey, but doesn't obey the laws himself.

Over a period of time, with repetition, these negative examples will strongly influence children away from a life of faith, of obedience to God, or of respect for their parents.

In *I Timothy 4:12*, Paul writes that *example* (which denotes a pattern, mold, or model) is the key in determining respect or disrespect.

> Let no man despise thy youth; but be thou an example
> of the believers, in word, in conversation, in charity, in
> spirit, in faith, in purity.

The word *despise* means "to think against" and is the seed which will mature into rejection of a parent's instructions. Once parents allow the seed of despising to be planted, the harvest of rebellion cannot be far behind. Because of the sowing and reaping principle, we must make sure that our "at home" behavior and our outside conversation (behavior, manner of life) are consistent, demonstrating that we genuinely believe that God's Word says we are indeed citizens of heaven and not of this world. Jesus said in *Matthew 6:24* that we cannot have it both ways. We will either love and serve God, or we will love and serve this world. Trying to straddle the fence will detour our children.

The apostle Paul thought about the power of example in his own life (*2 Corinthians 11:1*). We also should be concerned enough about the accumulation principle of example that we take a good, hard look at all the words, actions, and attitudes we are displaying and make sure that the accumulation principle is working for our children with righteous examples and not against them with unrighteous ones.

The Purity of Example

We must ask ourselves this question, "If I really believed what I say, would I be doing what I'm doing?" Disbelieving actions communicate, especially to our children, that we do not really believe what we say we believe. An inconsistent example is a truly dangerous detour for our young people, often producing blatant rejection of the "religion" of their parents when they are old enough to do so.

Remember the old sayings, "What you do speaks so loudly that I can't hear what you are saying," "Your walk talks and your talk talks, but your walk talks louder than your talk talks," or "The lessons of life are more caught than taught." Those proverbs communicate the heart of this dangerous detour that is so damaging to young people while they are in their formative years.

I remember well, as a child growing up in my parents' home, a number of times my parents had been saving for something special they wanted to buy. Something else "special" came up at church for which an appeal was made—a building project, a new piano, or a missions need. I remember Mom and Dad talking it over in front of my brother and myself. The ultimate decision was to give to the Lord rather than spend it on their "savings goal." That decision spoke volumes to me about my parents' life goals and basic beliefs. And then when I knew the gift was given to the church anonymously, that spoke volumes to me about Mom and Dad's character and humility. Dad was never a preacher. He taught some Sunday school classes and Mom helped out with junior church and hospitality needs, but it was not their church life that channeled my brother and me into a life of full-time service for God; it was their home life, their persistent, consistent, positive testimony that if we truly seek the kingdom of God first in our life goals and patterns, all these other things will come later (*Matthew 6:33*).

We can learn from Paul's admonitions to the Philippian believers concerning his own example.

> *Philippians 3:17-19*—Brethren, be followers together of me, and mark them which walk so as ye have us for an ensample. (For many walk, of whom I have told you often, and now tell you even weeping, that they are the enemies of the cross of Christ: whose end is destruction,

whose God is their belly, and whose glory is in their shame, who mind earthly things.)

- *Brethren*—These verses address born-again believers.
- *Followers of me*—Paul was not afraid to tell people to follow his example, to do what he said and what he did.
- *Mark them*—*Strong's* says the word means, "to look at, observe, contemplate." Paul invites the believers to look at others, to think about what they are seeing, and to remember it.
- *Walk*—This word refers to one's manner of life, how one habitually lives.
- *Example*—Paul's life was a pattern to be imitated and followed; he was duplicating himself.

Children actually duplicate attitudes, values, goals, and purposes, and not just surface actions or behaviors. Thirty years ago, I heard an illustration at a conference that can help us understand this thought.

A fairly successful businessman had worked his whole life to accumulate enough money to retire on, and, just before he was able to achieve his goal, his son, acting in what most people would label "rebellion," became a hippie. The businessman asked, "How could it be true that a son imitates his father when the father had worked hard all his life and his own son, as soon as he got a chance, gave up work and became a loafer? The answer is very simple. The dad, who had worked his whole life to retire as a legitimate loafer, had a son who beat him to retirement, not out of rebellion, but from patterning his life after what he saw really motivating his father.

That story may be a little stretched, but it illustrates the basic truth that what is genuinely important in a parent's life, not what he says is important, is what the children will grasp and imitate. We need to take a good, hard look at our values, which are revealed clearly by our attitudes and actions, and then honestly judge whether or not they are the same as those we verbalize. If we don't make this evaluation, we run the risk of raising worldly, materialistic children in a "Christian" home. Our Lord said, "No man can serve two masters . . ." *(Matthew 6:24a).* If we verbalize our love for the Lord but the example of our life is basically materialistic, what is the real message received by our children?

The Precepts of Example

How can I make sure the power of example is working for me and not against me? The key is found in *Philippians 4:9.*

> Those things, which ye have both learned, and received, and heard, and seen in me, do...

In this verse, the apostle Paul admonishes the believers to follow his own personal example. There are three key precepts in this verse that can instruct us concerning the power of example.

Key Precept #1—The verse we are looking at starts with learning and ends with doing. Educators often define learning as a change in behavior. For example, if a child learns the multiplication tables, he will more likely multiply than add items one at a time. When asked to count the number of tiles on the floor, he could number them one by one, or he could add the number of tiles in the length and the width and multiply them together for the total number of tiles. That change of behavior would indicate that he has learned multiplication. The goal of teaching is that the student will use what he has learned. Example's influence begins with a goal (learning) and ends with the results (doing).

Key Precept #2—Students only learn what they decide to receive. Receiving means to take or accept unto oneself as on accepts with the mind the instruction of teachers." If, when a child says in his mind, "that's right; I agree with that," instead of rejecting the instruction by saying "no" to it in his head, then learning will take place. If, on the other hand, his mind rejects the truth being taught, then there may be outward conformity to eliminate conflict, but inside the rejection will prevent genuine learning. Such outward conformity will extend only to the limits of parental reach.

Key Precept #3—This final precept comes from the phrase, "heard and seen in me." Remember the adage, "What you do speaks so loud that I can't hear what you are saying." What we do (that which our children see) must be consistent with what we say (that which our children hear). If the two agree, the likelihood of "receiving" increases and real internal learning results, producing a change in behavior (growth). If the two disagree, children will reject inconsistency and if they learn anything from inconsistent parents, it will be how to put on a good front the way Mom and Dad do! And, if they learn to be "good hypocrites," we may never know what they really believe until they move out of our homes.

We thus see that our children doing what we have taught them is contingent on their mentally "receiving" or accepting as truth our teaching, and that acceptance is in turn based upon our example (actions and lifestyle) being consistent with our words. So, is *example* our friend or our foe? If it is our foe, we have, without realizing it, sent our children on a detour that ends in the land of *Rejectus-Hipocritus*. How much better to make example our friend and ally for the journey ahead, thus helping our children to stay on the right road, to the right destination.

Companion Passages:

Philippians 2—Four illustrations of the example of a life being used to challenge and teach

1 Corinthians 11:1; 1 Timothy 4:12; Ephesians 5:1-2; 1 Peter 2:18-21; 2 Timothy 3:10, 14-15—Verses dealing with being an example to others in one's life

1 Corinthians 10:1-12—Using the examples found in the Scriptures as a teaching tool

Discussion Questions:

1. The power behind example is the power of _____ _____.

2. Discuss various ways that we can undermine what we are trying to teach by the way we act and live.

3. The root word for example refers to the making of a _____ _____ or a mold from which objects are formed, just like the original.

4. Which Bible character is the most positive example and challenge to you personally?

5. Which person living during your lifetime has been the greatest positive example? Why?

6. Explain *Philippians 4:9* in your own words.

7. What examples from your past have had a long-term effect upon you? For good? For bad? Why?

6

DETOUR

SIX

*Let your conversation be without coveteousness;
and be content with such things as ye have:
for he hath said, I will never leave thee,
nor forsake thee.*
Hebrews 13:5

DOMINATING DISCONTENTMENT

Coveteousness, which is idolatry.
Colossians 3:5b

*Let your conversation be without
coveteousness; and be content with such
things as ye have: for he hath said, I will
never leave thee, nor forsake thee.*
Hebrews 13:5

*He that is greedy of gain troubleth his
own house; but he that hateth gifts shall live.*
Proverbs 15:27

Wow!!! Did you detect the danger is those three verses? First, God considers covetousness to be the same as idolatry, as people bowing down before and worshipping pagan gods. Second, He says that to refuse contentment and choose covetousness is to ignore His promise never to leave us or forsake us. A covetous person is guilty of the sin of unbelief, of either assuming that God doesn't care about us, or that He is unable to care for us. Third, the Scriptures point out the trouble that greed will bring to a family, the kind of trouble which "stirs the pot" and encourages all kinds of problems and emotions that were better left alone. You've probably heard the saying, "Let sleeping dogs lie." Well, greed and covetousness stir up the dirty dogs of our weak fleshly nature, which will, in turn, bring great spiritual hardships upon the very ones we are trying to provide for. Ironically, in most cases, God would do for us what we are striving to do for ourselves if we would just obey His commands concerning material things and then let Him bless us as He sees fit. (*Proverbs 10:22*—"The blessing of the LORD, it maketh rich, and he addeth no sorrow with it.")

Contentment Defined

The Scriptures very clearly require believers to "be content" in this world. But what is contentment? *Webster's 1828 Dictionary* defines *contentment* as "a rest or quietness of the mind in the present condition; satisfaction, which holds the mind in peace, restraining complaint, opposition, or further desire, and often implying a moderate degree of happiness."

Contentment is an attitude of confidence in God's adequate provision, His loving goodness and kindness, and His giving nature, having already provided the most precious gift of all, His Son.

1 Timothy 6:17b says to not trust in riches "but in the living God, who giveth us richly all things to enjoy." In essence, contentment is a trust in God, and covetousness is a doubting of God. Contentment is not complacency; the Scriptures consistently teach us to work hard, avoid slothfulness (laziness), and be good stewards through savings and investment. But we should exercise our stewardship responsibilities within the context of biblical values, goals, and priorities. As *Matthew 6:33* reminds us, "But seek ye first the kingdom of God, and his righteousness; and all these things shall be added unto you."

Covetousness Defined

The covetous person has forfeited contentment for things. *Webster's 1828 Dictionary* defines *covetous* as being "inordinately desirous; excessively eager to obtain and possess." It is a strong inner desire to acquire more, an insatiable desire for gain, and easily leads to the sins of envy and greed. Ultimately, covetousness produces idolatry as Paul teaches in *Colossians 3:5*, "Mortify therefore your members which are upon the earth; fornication, uncleanness, inordinate affection, evil concupiscence, and covetousness, which is idolatry." He repeats this connection in *Ephesians 5:5*, "For this ye know, that no whoremonger, nor unclean person, nor covetous man, who is an idolater, hath any inheritance in the kingdom of Christ and of God." God views an inordinate drive to acquire more and more without considering Him the sin of idolatry.

God's condemnation of this particular sin is clear because He forbids it in the Ten Commandments, written on stone with His own finger, and are God's first written revelation to man. There are only ten of them, and they are indeed key components in our relationship with God and with one another. In *Exodus 20:17*, the Scripture says, "Thou shalt not covet thy neighbor's house, thou shalt not covet thy neighbor's wife, nor his manservant, nor his maidservant, nor his ox, nor his ass, nor any thing that is thy neighbor's." In this command God says we can be guilty of covetousness in the following areas of:

- Our housing
- Our spouses
- Our lifestyle (servants)
- Our tools and equipment (ox)
- Our cars and vehicles (ass)

So, the motivation of covetousness can be a desire for either material things or for alternative relationships or both. We must be on guard against these twin dangers in our hearts. They have the potential of destroying us and our marriages, and they can detour our children off the road of God's will and blessing. Which of the following lists of synonyms would you want used to describe your family?

Covetous	**Content**
Avaricious	Satisfied
Insatiable	Sufficient
Greedy	Happy
Materialistic	Comfortable
Miserly	Pleased
Stingy	Fulfilled
Selfish	Peaceful

There is more behind the sin of covetousness than just wanting more than I now have. When this desire is tied to wrong motivations, pride, and a lack of trust in the Savior, the desire is transformed into the sinful detour of covetousness. Discontentment is not simply wanting to improve our lives by doing what is reasonable to work toward that end. Scripture never censures initiative and industry, but it does condemn laziness. This dangerous detour embodies five issues of great consequence for the members of our family. These are issues that can transform industry and initiative into self-serving covetousness.

1. The issue of **disloyalty**—acting as though God cannot meet our needs and provide for our necessities and turning to the world to provide peace and happiness for us.

    Philippians 4:19—But my God shall supply all your need according to his riches in glory by Christ Jesus.

    James 4:4—Ye adulterers and adulteresses, know ye not that the friendship of the world is enmity with God? Whosoever therefore will be a friend of the world is the enemy of God.

2. The issue of **wrong values or purposes for our life**—

acquiring man-centered or me-centered goals instead of living under God-centered priorities.

Matthew 6:33—But seek ye first the kingdom of God, and his righteousness; and all these things shall be added unto you.

3. The issue of an **unwillingness to sacrifice for God**— saying "no" to God, always a dangerous decision for a family. This is not a request for sacrifice above and beyond the call of duty, but rather it is referred to as our reasonable service.

    Romans 12:1-2— I beseech you therefore, brethren, by the mercies of God, that ye present your bodies a living sacrifice, holy, acceptable unto God, *which is* your reasonable service. And be not conformed to this world: but be ye transformed by the renewing of your mind, that ye may prove what *is* that good, and acceptable, and perfect, will of God.

4. The issue of **unfruitfulness for God**—failing to control ourselves, producing a life cluttered with the "thorny things" of materialism so that we become unfruitful pseudo-servants of the Lord, unable at best and unwilling at worst to serve Him.

    Matthew 13:22—He also that received seed among the thorns is he that heareth the word; and the care of this world, and the deceitfulness of riches, choke the word, and he becometh unfruitful.

5. The issue of **doubting God**
    *   By thinking that, in order to get what we want, we must do what we think God is obviously not doing for us.

Sometimes we actually become angry with God when we don't get what we feel we need or deserve.

Exodus 17:1-7— And all the congregation of the children of Israel journeyed from the wilderness of Sin, after their journeys, according to the commandment of the LORD, and pitched in Rephidim: and *there was* no water for the people to drink. Wherefore the people did chide with Moses, and said, Give us water that we may drink. And Moses said unto them, Why chide ye with me? Wherefore do ye tempt the LORD? And the people thirsted there for water; and the people murmured against Moses, and said, Wherefore *is* this *that* thou hast brought us up out of Egypt, to kill us and our children and our cattle with thirst? And Moses cried unto the LORD, saying, What shall I do unto this people? They be almost ready to stone me. And the LORD said unto Moses, Go on before the people, and take with thee of the elders of Israel; and thy rod, wherewith thou smotest the river, take in thine hand, and go. Behold, I will stand before thee there upon the rock in Horeb; and thou shalt smite the rock, and there shall come water out of it, that the people may drink. And Moses did so in the sight of the elders of Israel. And he called the name of the place Massah, and Meribah, because of the chiding of the children of Israel, and because they tempted the LORD, saying, Is the LORD among us, or not?

- By not believing His promises regarding giving and receiving—not believing that God can bring blessing as He promised.

> *Luke 6:38*—Give, and it shall be given unto you, good measure, pressed down, and shaken together, and running over, shall men give into your bosom. For with the same measure that ye mete withal it shall be measured to you again.

If any of these five issues become the standard operating procedure for someone in our family or for our family as a whole, then a dangerous detour leading toward long-term heartache and hurt has been taken (*1 Timothy 6:8-10).*

Ways We Can Doubt God with Covetous Attitudes

If we are not content, but rather covetous, then we doubt God by not believing Him; and then rather than resting in His promise, we question His character. Let's examine the following two passages of Scripture in a little more detail:

> *Hebrews 13:5*—**Let your conversation be without covetousness; and be content with such things as ye have: for he hath said, I will never leave thee, nor forsake thee.**

... for He hath said...—Is He truthful, accurate, and sincere in His words? Are they accurately recorded for us in Scripture (inspiration)? The *foundation of our very faith* is at stake if we doubt God's integrity.

... I will...—Does God really want to provide for my needs? Is He able? Will He do me good and not harm? Is He paying attention to my prayers? Does He know my problems? The *confidence of our faith* is at stake if we doubt God's sovereignty.

... never leave thee...—Does He really care about me, per-

sonally? Will He get tired of meeting my needs? Is He dependable? Is He strong enough to care for me, individually, when there are so many other needs to deal with in the world? The *endurance of our faith* is at stake if we doubt God's faithfulness.

... nor forsake thee...—Will He really always be with me? What if He gets tired of me and leaves or puts His attention someplace else? Will He leave me on my own just to teach me a lesson? The *freedom of our faith* is at stake if we doubt God's commitment.

Covetousness also destroys confidence in God and creates uncertainty through doubt. We find another promise of God in *1 Peter*.

> *1 Peter 5:7*—**Casting all your care upon him; for he careth for you.**

... casting all...—Does God really mean *all*? The *basis of our faith* is at stake when we doubt God's truthfulness.

... your care...—Does He want all my anxious fears given to Him? The *depth of our faith* is at stake when we doubt God's sincerity.

... for He careth for you...— Does He really care? We may say, "I know Scripture says He loves me, but does He really care?" The *joy of our faith* is at stake when we doubt God's heart.

Testing My Contentment

Slipping from an attitude of contentment into a lifestyle of covetousness is neither swift nor dramatic. A little change here, a little change there, and before we realize it, greed has a driving grip on our life so that we act in ways we never thought possible.

Are we, without realizing it, putting up the detour sign of discontentment and as parents modeling a lifestyle that undermines the trust of our children in a loving Savior Who has said that He would "supply all your need according to His riches in glory by Christ Jesus" *(Philippians 4:19)?* Perhaps we need to check our "contentment quotient." Giving honest answers to the following questions will provide the score.

1. What if I never have any more than I have now? Could I be happy?
2. Do I want what others have just because someone else has it?
3. How long has it been since I expressed thankfulness to God or others? *2 Corinthians 9:15*
4. Does it always take one more thing to make me happy? Where is my focus?
5. After acquiring something I've desired for a long while, do I immediately start wanting something else?
6. Do I constantly worry about the future?
7. Do I worry, fret, or refuse to give to others or to the Lord because I might not have enough for myself? *2 Corinthians 8:1-15*
8. How do I handle the surplus God puts in my hands? Am I willing to give and to give cheerfully? *2 Corinthians 9:6-8*
9. Do money worries keep me awake at night?
10. Is my consumer debt larger than my monthly income?

Road to Contentment
If, after reading over this list of questions, we discern that we are traveling on this detour of discontentment and want to get back on the right road, we must take the following sequential steps:

1. Confess our sin of covetousness to the Lord (*1 John 1:9*).

2. Ask God for help in learning contentment as the apostle Paul learned it in *Philippians 4:11-13:*

Not that I speak in respect of want: for I have learned, in whatsoever state I am, therewith to be content. I know both how to be abased, and I know how to abound: everywhere and in all things I am instructed both to be full and to be hungry, both to abound and to suffer need. I can do all things through Christ which strengtheneth me.

- Paul *learned* contentment; it is not a trait some people are born with and others are not. We can learn it, too! Contentment is a learned skill and attitude.
- Those at both ends of the material spectrum need to learn to be content. It is often harder for the wealthy because they can more easily get what they think they want and because they have more to lose.
- Contentment is a skill and attitude that require the strength of God; we cannot acquire contentment without God's grace.

3. Study and meditate on *1 Timothy 6:6-19*, looking for the three keys to being "content with such things as ye have."

1 Timothy 6:6-19—But godliness with contentment is great gain. For we brought nothing into *this* world, *and it is* certain we can carry nothing out. And having food and raiment let us be therewith content. But they that will be rich fall into temptation and a snare, and *into* many foolish and hurtful lusts, which drown men in destruction and perdition. For the love of money is the root of all evil: which while some coveted after, they have erred from the faith, and pierced themselves through with many sorrows. But thou, O man of God, **flee** these things; and **follow** after righteousness, godliness, faith, love, patience, meekness. **Fight** the good fight of faith, lay hold on eternal life, whereunto thou art also called, and hast professed a good profession before many witnesses. I give thee charge in the sight of God, who quickeneth all things, and *before* Christ Jesus, who before Pontius Pilate witnessed a good confession; that thou keep *this* commandment without spot, unrebukable, until the appearing of our Lord Jesus Christ: which in his times he shall show, *who is* the blessed and only Potentate, the King of kings, and Lord of lords; who only hath immortality, dwelling in the light which no man can approach unto; whom no man hath seen, nor can see: to whom *be* honor and power everlasting. Amen. Charge them that are rich in this world, that they be not highminded; nor trust in uncertain riches, but in the living God, who giveth us richly all things to enjoy; that they do good, that they be rich in good works, ready to distribute, willing to communicate; laying up in store for themselves a good foundation against the time to come, that they may lay hold on eternal life.

This passage reveals Paul's instruction to Timothy concerning learning contentment. If we really want to learn contentment, we must spend significant time in this passage, meditating on it, and asking the Lord to instruct us personally, by His strength, to deal with covetousness. Living in such an overwhelmingly materialistic society, we must diligently study and learn from the Word in order to keep our focus toward God.

The Three Keys—Flee, Follow, and Fight

We must flee (to move away from) two things. First, we must flee from a "will" to be rich as our primary goal in life. Then we must flee from the "love of money," which is the temptation to believe that money can do for us what God desires to do for us.

We must **follow**, or pursue as a manner of life, the things God would want us to have, knowing that they bring true happinesss and joy in life.

- Righteousness—right living as a child of God
- Godliness—pursuing a godly lifestyle with Christ as our example
- Faith—belief in what the Bible says so that we act upon it
- Love—self-sacrificing desire to meet the needs of another
- Patience—steadfast, not swerving from purpose, endurance
- Meekness—accepting all of God's dealing with me (even bad times) as good

We must **fight**. Fleeing and following are not enough; God also wants us to fight the "good fight of faith." To truly live by faith is always a struggle. On the other hand, it is so easy to give lip service to faith and then do it all ourselves. Here at Ironwood, we call this the "Walt Factor." That's when we know what God wants us to do and then I hatch some idea on how we can earn enough to pay for it. All along God not only wants us to do His will, but He also wants to pay for it through His miracle-working power and grace. Every time we have gone the "Walt Factor" route, we, and me in particular, have encountered much heartache and sorrow as I learn anew to trust God. So what are we to fight? We are to fight three attitudes: haughtiness and pride, thinking we can do this ourselves; idolatrous confidence in what the Scriptures call "uncertain riches"; and selfishness which destroys our desire to willingly give to the Lord and share with others. The result of all this fleeing, following, and fighting is the laying up of a good foundation for life both for now and for eternity.

Bible-Wise Family Finances

One third or more of all marriage problems revolve around money and how it is spent, wasted, saved, invested, or mishandled by family members. Two thirds of the parables deal with financial matters and principles. God has truly given us "all things richly to enjoy," but like all of God's gifts to man, using them incorrectly or getting them out of balance creates problems. Money can be used properly or the love of money can become the root of all evil. If we want to live within the context of God's blessing on our lives, we must learn, submit to, and obey the basic Bible principles God has established for His people.

Bible Laws Regarding Finances

1. We cannot serve (love) both God and money. *Matthew 6:24*
   - Refers to life purposes, goals, and priorities
   - Revealed by the choices we make. *Hebrews 11:25*

2. We must not trust in money, but in the living God. *1 Timothy 6:17*
   - Refers to our search for security and provision.
   - Reveals whether our value system is temporal or eternal. *Matthew 16:26*

3. We must remember that we are but stewards of God's wealth. (He owns it all - *Psalm 24:1*.) *Matthew 25:14-19*
   - Refers to the source of wealth, even the power to earn wealth. *Deuteronomy 8:18*
   - Reveals our accounting to God for our proper handling of all He has given us. *1 Timothy 6:17-19; Philippians 4:17-18; Romans 14:12*

4. We must control our attitudes regarding material things. *Hebrews 13:5; 1 Timothy 3:3; 6:6-8*

- Refers to our contentment with what God has provided in His love.
- Reveals that proper priorities do not mean doing without. *Matthew 6:33*

5. We must remember by faith that it is better to give than to receive. *Acts 20:35*
   - Refers to the eternal values that we must not only espouse, but also act upon. *Matthew 6:19-21*
   - Reveals God's blessing for remembering that all we have is God's and His way is to bless those who give from what little they have to others in need. *Luke 6:38; Philippians 4:17,19*

6. We should make active lifestyle choices and settle for a "living-by-default" attitude. *2 Peter 3:11; Hebrews 11:24-27*
   - Refers to our duty to make plans within the context of God's will. *James 4:13-15*
   - Reveals that a good financial plan is pleasing to the Lord as long as we don't become self-sufficient. *Luke 11:3; 12:21; 14:28*

Materialism and the discontentment it brings severely harms many families by dictating their life goals, by robbing them of their family time, and by handicapping their relationships. Many young people in Christian homes today view a good education and a college degree as only a means to a good paying job, and not as a means to an opportunity to serve and contribute. This says something about the prevalence of a great big detour sign that says, "Covetousness, turn in here."

Contentment requires diligence. Covetousness is easy and the road most followed by our society. But if God's way is our choice, our best plan is to study and meditate on the Scriptures mentioned in this chapter and then seek, through the help of the Holy Spirit, to live our life by them. The Bible study on "Learning Contentment" in the Appendix may be helpful in understanding this issue, in getting off the detour route, and in beginning the journey on the road of contentment. Victory is possible by following God's Word, but if we do not choose to apply His Word in our life, this detour will undermine the very foundation of our family.

Companion Passages:
Luke 6:46-48—What is the difference between a good foundation and a poor foundation?
Matthew 6:33-34; Luke11:34-36: 12:22-34—Verses from the teaching of Christ dealing with materialism.
Psalm 78—a Psalm recounting how God cared for the Israelites in the wilderness and how they still continued to sin and doubt Him.
Psalm 106:13-15
Proverbs 30:7-9

Discussion and Study Questions:
1. What is the tenth commandment (*Exodus 20:1-17*), and how does it relate to being discontent?

2. In *Colossians 3:5* covetousness is listed as being equal to
_____.

3. How can covetousness be considered by God to be disloyal to Himself?

4. How did the apostle Paul have the strength to learn contentment in his own life? See *Philippians 4:11-13*.

5. Why/how do you suppose it is possible to be serving God today and not tomorrow? See *Matthew 13:22*.

6. How can following the qualities mentioned in *1 Timothy 6:11* help us deal with covetousness?

7. Is it possible to not be covetous and still not be content? Explain your answer.

7

DETOUR
SEVEN

See then that ye walk circumspectly, not as fools,
but as wise, redeeming the time, because the days
are evil. Wherefore be ye not unwise, but
understanding what the will of the Lord is.
Ephesians 5:15-17

DISTRACTED PARENTS

See then that ye walk circumspectly, not as fools,
but as wise, redeeming the time, because the days
are evil. Wherefore be ye not unwise, but
understanding what the will of the Lord is.
Ephesians 5:15-17

It is hard to imagine a time in history when people have had more options on their plates than they do now. Some of those choices seem to be perceived today as necessities, when, just a few years ago they would have been "far out" luxuries...things like internet access, weekend RV trips, or selecting which football game to "not" watch from the options the satellite dish brings into our homes. Add to these choices the fact that the average household is now supported by 2.5 full-time jobs, and we have provided a devastating detour for our children. Time has become a very rare commodity in the average household, and this phenomenon communicates loudly to our children. I have never read a book or an article on how to demonstrate love that did not include as one of the indispensable evidences of love, the spending of a significant amount of quality time with the ones we love. In *Ephesians 5:15-17* Paul gives several imperatives that wise parents will heed:

> See then that ye walk circumspectly, not as fools, but as wise. Redeeming the time, because the days are evil. Wherefore be ye not unwise, but understanding what the will of the Lord is.

As we look at these three verses, let's remember that the most precious things in our earthly life are our family members. They alone are eternal among all the "things" and "organizations" that surround us; only people will live forever. Therefore, our family should occupy a significant place on our list of important ways to spend our time. The trouble is that we are too busy sorting through the clutter of apparently urgent things to give our families their truly important place in our lives.

Wise or Foolish Parenting

Ephesians 5:15-17 tells us that the use of our time indicates whether we are parenting *wisely* (in a way that pleases God and lays up treasure for eternity) or *foolishly* (as if there were no God or any accounting of our time upon this earth). To parent *foolishly* is to believe that how we use our time now has little or no consequences with our children and the choices they will make.

Time can be redeemed. The *Webster's 1828 Dictionary* defines *redeem* as "to purchase back," "to repurchase what has been sold," "to save," and "to redeem time is to use more diligence in the improvement of it; to be diligent and active in duty and preparation." Although we cannot buy back spent time, we can buy back all the time left today, which will have an impact on tomorrow. Time is like money in that we can spend it today, but it is unlike money in that we cannot save it for the future. When we save time, we are using or spending it wisely, getting more accomplished in the same amount of time. We cannot take two unused hours from today and save them for another day's use. To parent *wisely* is to redeem the time by doing the most important things first not allowing ourselves to be dominated by all the urgent voices.

The purpose for redeeming the time is because the days (times we live in) are evil (full of labors, annoyances, hardships, and wickedness) and full of peril to our Christian faith and steadfastness. Choices for how we spend our time continue to grow, and the choices for evil seem to multiply many times faster than our choices for good. To parent *foolishly* is to parent as if there were no hard choices to make, no battles to fight, and no orders from God to obey.

So how do distracted parents post dangerous detours for their children? If we parent *foolishly,* we will not have the necessary discernment to train or teach our children in eternally-significant ways. They may learn how to become financially prosperous and successful, but what about eternal treasures? Learning biblical discernment demands time and effort. To parent *wisely* is to spend the time necessary to "understand what the will of the Lord is."

If we parent *foolishly* and not spend the quantity and quality of time necessary to show our children our love, they may spend the rest of their lives seeking that security and love from others. Children who cannot resist peer pressure, and who, as teens, desperately seek the approval of peers have not experienced the needed unconditional family love. Parents, who become so preoccupied with their jobs, hobbies, and daily problems that they don't spend enough time to truly know their children, will nudge their children onto a detour. This alternate route is a difficult road often demonstrating no resistance to peer pressure or immoral behavior such as pre-marital sex. Studies show that the lack of a father's love is a major contributor to a daughter becoming promiscuous.

Although we are primarily addressing parents concerning time with their children, our love for our spouse is communicated in much the same way through time spent. Fathers often focus on their job to the neglect of their family, including their wife; mothers often focus on the children to the neglect of their husbands. Both are distracting detours to the security of the child. We must demonstrate to our children a dynamic husband/wife relationship that is always growing and improving. We parent *foolishly* when the husband and wife neglect their relationship, and as a result, a child-centered home often develops. The role of being a parent is placed above the role of husband or wife. The distraction element here is not about a parent being distracted and a child being neglected, but about a parent being distracted from his or her most important role, that of being a loving spouse, and a child being deprived of one of his greatest needs—a two-parent home full of love. Such child-centered homes feed the selfish nature of children and often end with children being spoiled brats, thinking the whole universe should revolve around them and their desires.

Practical Principles for Wise Parenting

1. Just because we can does not mean we should. Maybe we don't need to take that promotion that will keep us away from home more just as our children are becoming teenagers and will need our time more than ever. Some things just should not be done.

2. Requests always exceed resources. We must learn to say "NO!" I've spent my life saying "yes" to God and to ministry opportunities, but when my children hit a certain age, I had to learn to say "no" to some opportunities. Did it hurt my ministry? Well, I don't believe Ironwood grew as much as it could have during those years, but my children are all in full-time ministry today. I once saw a plaque hanging in a restaurant that said "the squeaking wheel gets the grease, but

the quacking duck gets shot."Yes, there are some urgencies that need some grease, but there are others that just need to be eliminated.

3. The *urgent* is always the enemy of the *important*. We must not neglect the eternal *important* for the cry of the *urgent* of today...no matter how loud it gets. We must not fall for the devil's lie that the most important thing we can do for our children is to provide for them financially. When parents are so distracted by good things like jobs, hobbies, yards, etc., or by urgent things like constant calls from work, that they fail in spending the necessary time on the important things, their children will end up on a dangerous detour. Important things in life have eternal consequences and must not be neglected because of the urgent. Our personal relationship with our Lord, our love relationship with our spouse, and our time with our children must be "redeemed." Time with our children is not only time spent in activities with them; it is time spent thinking about their needs, praying for them, teaching them, working with them, and disciplining and admonishing them. We must not get distracted from the *important*.

4. Choices of how to spend time should be measured by the durability factor, which is how long our various choices will last. The answer could be anywhere from a few seconds to our whole life, and ultimately, choices could be eternal. Durability helps us to determine value. When we have choices before us, we should consider which will have the greatest value for eternity.

5. The *past neglect, present need* formula will help us decide if we need to spend more time with our loved ones.

Past Neglect—Has there been some neglect in the past that needs to be made up for now? Past neglect can probably never be totally balanced, but a makeup of such times helps. When there has been some neglect in the past, more time needs to be allotted in the present.

Present Need—Your teenage daughter is feeling unloved now because she just got braces and some of the teens are making fun of her. Instead of Dad telling her to "tough it out," perhaps he needs to spend a little extra time with her and reaffirm his love. There are so many situations where a present need seems to be demanding attention. Real discernment is required to apply biblical and practical principles and quickly decide how to spend the next few hours of our life.

We need to figure out a "standard of value" (an economic term for one of the functions of money) for the use of our time. What in our life is very important and enjoyable? Maybe it takes half a day. Now, each time we have half a day and a choice of activities, we need to measure our choices again by our "time standard of value" and see how important each of our various choices really are.

Only one life will soon be past;
Only what's done for Christ will last.

Our culture is feeding us a big lie. It is saying "things" make us happy and money is what we need to get more things. They would have us believe that getting two jobs (or working the equivalent in overtime) so we can "provide" more things for our children is the way to prove or show our love. That is just not true. Children spell love—T-I-M-E. If we as parents are distracted for one good reason or another and do not spend the necessary time with each of our children, they will be detoured around some of the really best "things" in life.

Time usage is all a matter of establishing priorities in our life. What really is of greatest value to us will be shown in the choices we make.

Companion Scriptures Passages:
James 4:13-17
Luke 14:25-35
Matthew 6:25-34
Philippians 3:13-14
Colossians 3

Discussion and Study Questions:

1. What do you think would be a good definition of time?

2. What is a distraction?

3. How have you learned to prioritize your life/time?

4. How do children spell LOVE? ___ ___ ___ ___

5. Why should we redeem the time or even consider it to be important?

6. What does *redeem* mean?

7. How is time like/unlike money?

8

DETOUR EIGHT

*Be careful for nothing; but in every thing by prayer
and supplication with thanksgiving let your requests
be made known unto God. And the peace of God, which
passeth all understanding, shall keep your hearts and
minds through Christ Jesus.*

Philippians 4:6-7

Deliberate Despair

Be careful for nothing; but in every thing by prayer and supplication with thanksgiving let your requests be made known unto God. And the peace of God, which passeth all understanding, shall keep your hearts and minds through Christ Jesus.
Philippians 4:6-7

Negative thinking destroys ambition, hope, and peace of mind; such thinking is the access road parents often take to reach the destination of despair. I have labeled this despair deliberate because believers choose negative thinking. When you see a half a glass of water, do you think of it as half full or half empty? Looking at the gloomy, dark, and pessimistic side of life strikes a terrible blow to our faith in a sovereign, all-knowing, good, loving, and righteous God. Christians who are constantly fearful and anxious are "unbelieving" believers who exhibit doubt in God's compassion, knowledge, or ability to answer prayer. *Philippians 4:6-7* commands us,

> Be careful for nothing; but in every thing by prayer and supplication with thanksgiving, let your requests be made known unto God. And the peace of God, which passeth all understanding, shall keep your hearts and minds through Christ Jesus.

Negative thinking denies the truth of these verses and paves the way to the detour of despair.

Paul's words to the Philippian Christians imply that the circumstances and problems of life, when viewed from a natural perspective, could cause believers to become anxious and fearful; instead, we need to consider life and situations from a spiritual point of view. To view life from this perspective is a choice we must be making continually, as we face challenging circumstances. First, we should take the matter to the Lord in prayer, thanking Him as we pray about this "new opportunity" to trust Him. Then, as we receive the "peace of God" in our heart, we need to look deliberately at our options for dealing with the opportunity and/or problem and select the one that will please the Lord. Sometimes our best response is to do nothing and just wait on the Lord. Sometimes, God's will involves a choice that requires hard work, but it does not include a choice where a negative attitude of griping, complaining, blaming others, or questioning God's goodness for our circumstances is permissible.

When we first recognize our tendency toward negative thinking (an easy habit to fall into), we will be tempted to rationalize the thoughts as "no big deal." That response would be a dangerous maneuver for us and also for the children who are growing up and learning how to handle life from us. Negativity boils down to how much we believe God and what kind of example of faith we are living in front of our children. We may preach the gospel of faith, but if we live the gospel of despair, it is that gospel our children will believe.

Are there any who could legitimately feel despair and become discouraged? Should a Christian ever succumb to such feelings? I know that we often have real problems that appear to have no viable solutions. However, our faith in God's goodness should sustain and strengthen us to thank and praise Him even in the midst of great difficulties. Although we may slip at times in despair's direction, our faith in God and His Word should keep us from going too far down the path of this detour. In reality, only those without saving faith in Christ Jesus should be living a life of despair, hopelessness, or fear. The Bible says in *Ephesians 2:12* concerning the Ephesians before their conversion, "That at that time ye were without Christ…having no hope, and without God in the world." The unsaved are firmly on that detour of despair. Although many of them have figured out ways to put on a good front, or have embraced some philosophy of life or pseudo-religion in the hopes of finding peace—at the end of the day, and in the silence of their hearts, they will find no peace without Jesus Christ. It would be a real tragedy if believers, who have no reason to be in the depths of despair, were to be as full of eternally empty despair as unbelievers are.

When Christians find themselves on this detour, they are exhibiting either a lack of faith in God or a lack of knowledge of God and of His nature and power. Reading, studying, and believing such passages as *Romans 8:31-39* should certainly give us the confidence to live without the anxious fear and hopelessness that leads to despair.

> What shall we then say to these things? If God be for us, who can be against us? He that spared not his own Son, but delivered him up for us all, how shall he not with him also freely give us all things? Who shall lay any thing to the charge of God's elect? It is God that justifieth. Who is he that condemneth? It is Christ that died, yea rather, that is risen again, who is even at the right hand of God, who also maketh intercession for us. Who shall separate us from the love of Christ? Shall tribulation, or distress, or persecution, or famine, or nakedness, or peril, or sword? As it is written, For thy sake we are killed all the day long; we are accounted as sheep for the slaughter. Nay, in all these things we are

127

more than conquerors through him that loved us. For I
am persuaded, that neither death, nor life, nor angels,
nor principalities, nor powers, nor things present, nor
things to come, nor height, nor depth, nor any other
creature, shall be able to separate us from the love of
God, which is in Christ Jesus our Lord.

In this passage of Scripture we are challenged to think right!
God has already given us the "grand prize," the gift of His Son;
there is no reason to think He will not also provide the lesser
blessings of life as well. He has no reason to hold anything back
that is good for us and in His will. Nor can anything separate
us from His love, the same love that motivated Him to give His
Son (*John 3:16*). Some Christians act as if they think the evils
listed in the above passage are capable of separating us from the
love of God. But they cannot. Consider this list in the context
of today's world and society.

Bible Term	Today's Context
Tribulation	Hard, difficult times caused by forces we can't control, such as terrorists, floods, or fire.
Distress	Emotional turmoil that could suddenly surround and engulf us. Stress brought on by death, disease, divorce, deceit, etc.
Persecution	Heartache and trials brought to us just because of what we believe.
Famine	Today's terms would be economic trouble, national recession or depression, lay-offs, and double-digit unemployment rates.

Peril	Living in an unsafe environment of crime, terrorists, AIDS, accidents, etc.
Sword	A state of war which creates a whole category of distress all its own: personal loss and danger, potential loss of loved ones, loss of sense of security, etc.

Can any of these separate us from God's love? No, in "all these things we are more than conquerors through Him that loved us." Actually when these negative situations are spoken of in Scripture, God was active in using them to bring His people back to Himself.

Despair can be exhibited in a number of ways, but the way that most affects our children is the training by example to develop a negative thinking pattern. Constantly living with that kind of negative attitude is devastating to the future faith and well being of our families.

Seven Positive or Negative Choices
There are at least seven damaging attitudes that negative parents will be implanting in the minds of their children. *Proverbs 18:14* says that sooner or later anyone would succumb to a continual diet of negativity; "The spirit of man will sustain his infirmity; but a wounded spirit who can bear?" A person's ability to reject wrong thinking is limited, and negativity will eventually take its toll if allowed free reign in our hearts. So, what what is the effect on our children if, although we are saved, our life is characterized by negative thinking?

1. When, instead of an optimistic, **victorious attitude**, we sow despair, we will reap a **self-defeated** attitude in our children.

- Our children ought to have a "can do" spirit following the example of the apostle Paul when he said, "I can do all things through Christ which strengtheneth me" (*Philippians 4:13*). Children often have a habit of saying "I can't" even before they get started. "I can't" should not be in a family's vocabulary. The attitude one should have when faced with a difficult task is, "I am having difficulty and I may need help, but I can do this thing."

- Our children ought to have a confident attitude, understanding the truth of Paul's words. "But thanks be to God, which giveth us the victory through our Lord Jesus Christ" (*1 Corinthians 15:57*).

2. When, instead of **thankfulness** to God for all He has done for us, we sow ingratitude, we reap a **self-centered** attitude in our children.

- Our children ought to have a thankful, "others-first" love. *1 Corinthians 13* teaches us that love does not envy, seeks not his own, and hopes for all things. Do our children exhibit this kind of love when they see other kids get something new? A self-centered existence is filled with turmoil and selfish questions. "Who is going to do for me?" "What do I get out of it?"

- Our children ought to be a part of a family that is constantly thanking God for His graciousness and goodness. Notice the *always* and *all* in *Ephesians 5:20*, "Giving thanks always for all things unto God and the Father in the name of our Lord Jesus Christ."

3. When, instead of **peace**, we sow fear and anxiety, we will reap a **self-protective** attitude in our children.

- Our children ought to be able to trust in the goodness of God when fearful things come into their life, obeying Peter's advice, "Casting all your care upon him; for he careth for you" (*1 Peter 5:7*).

- Our children ought to see that trusting God brings peace, as *Isaiah 26:3* teaches us, "Thou wilt keep him in perfect peace, whose mind is stayed on thee: because he trusteth in thee." Insecure feelings and thoughts are replaced with a trust in God's love and care.

- Our children ought to be able to rely on God for their protection. Parents need to teach their children to prepare wisely and act prudently while applying the principle of *Proverbs 21:31*, "The horse is prepared against the day of battle, but safety is of the Lord." Prepare and pray, but in the end we must rely on God's protection. Living a life of constant fear and anxiety is a terrible detour to turn on.

4. When, instead of **contentment** in God's care "and with such things as ye have" (*Hebrews 13:5*), we sow covetousness and discontentment, we will reap a **self-absorbed** attitude in our children.

   - Our children ought to be learning the attitude of contentment as Paul did in *Philippians 4:11*, "Not that I speak in respect of want: for I have learned, in whatsoever state I am, therewith to be content." The opposite attitude is a self-focus of "I don't have what I deserve."

   - Our children ought to see the example of parents who are willing to care for others as Christ did and as Paul speaks of Timothy in *Philippians 2:20-21*, "For I have no

man likeminded, who will naturally care for your state.
For all seek their own, not the things which are Jesus
Christ's." When we live likeminded and our children
witness the blessing of God that follows, we will be
teaching the value of others-first loud and clear.

5. When, instead of **humility**, we sow proud, self-sufficiency,
we will reap a conceited, **self-promoting** attitude in our
children. This attitude is condemned by God and listed as
the primary characteristic of our sinful times. *2 Timothy
3:2*, "For men shall be lovers of their own selves, covetous,
boasters, proud, blasphemers, disobedient to parents, un-
thankful, unholy…" The tragedy of such pride is that once it
becomes a habit pattern in one's life, it is almost impossible
to convince that person that they do indeed have a problem.
He will almost always play the blame game.

   • Children ought not to be learning to be braggarts, boasters, and know-it-alls, but to be helpers and encouragers
of others. When our children were growing up, they
often entered ten or more events in the academic and
fine arts competitions at school each year; many more
than most students entered. They brought home ribbons
in most of the events and won many first-place awards.
They could have bragged about those legitimate achieve-
ments, but they didn't, because the rule in our house
was, "You can brag on yourself to Mom and Dad and to
each other, but you are never to brag to other kids or
put others down for their lack of achievement." I often
heard our children encouraging their friends to enter
more events and to do their best.

   • Children ought to be learning the principle of seeking
God first as in *Matthew 6:33,* "But seek ye first the king-

dom of God, and his righteousness; and all these things shall be added unto you." When we are allowing God to add the "things" of life, we will not be caught in the entrapment of devising ways to promote or provide for ourselves.

- Children ought to be learning the sufficiency of God instead of self-sufficiency. *2 Corinthians 3:5* tells us, "Not that we are sufficient of ourselves to think any thing as of ourselves; but our sufficiency *is* of God." This teaching will help our children as they may experience the despair of failure (and they will have failure), knowing that God is able to work through their weaknesses and not just their strengths.

- Children ought to learn to put aside their own desires in order to please others, as Paul told the Roman believers of this responsibility when he wrote, "We then that are strong ought to bear the infirmities of the weak, and not to please ourselves. Let every one of us please his neighbor for his good to edification. For even Christ pleased not himself..." (*Romans 15:1-3*).

6. When, instead of **living by faith**, trusting that God "is, and that he is a rewarder of them that diligently seek Him" (*Hebrews 11:6*), we try to do it all ourselves, we reap a **self-sufficient** attitude in our children. We have forgotten what God says in *John 15:5*, "without me ye can do nothing."

- Children ought to be learning to "walk by faith, not by sight" (*2 Corinthians 5:7*).

- Children ought to learn to work hard, but always remembering that God is working, too; in and through them. Although we may think our work-a-holism will teach them to work hard, more often the example of self-sufficiency will speak louder. *Colossians 1:29*, "Whereunto I also labor, striving according to his working, which worketh in me mightily."

7. When, instead of **trusting in the promise of God** "that all things work together for good" (*Romans 8:28*), we sow griping and complaining, we will reap a **self-pleasing** attitude in our children.

    • Children ought to be learning to "count it all joy" (*James 1:2-4*) when various kinds of trials come into their lives.

    • Children ought to be able to profit from seeing their own parents respond gratefully to negative things, thanking the Lord for them in obedience to Paul's instructions in *1 Thessalonians 5:18*, "In every thing give thanks: for this is the will of God in Christ Jesus concerning you."

    • Children ought to believe God's promises, and they will be much more likely to if they see their parents living the promises of God by faith.

Every one of these attitudes of the heart that children ought to possess are positive and upbeat in nature because they look to God for their expectations (*Psalm 62:5*). Children ought to have the benefit of such powerful expectations from God, but many children are deprived of such joy because of "unbelieving" Christian parents who live in despair.

Selfishness is the direct result of our negative attitude toward the people and circumstances in our lives. Such pride is often accompanied by anger, prayerlessness, destruction (*Proverbs 16:18*), contention (*Proverbs 13:10*), and ultimately, despair. What a terrible detour to lead our children onto. How much better it would be to live by faith in God, believing either that He will help us deal with and solve our opportunities/problems or that He will give us the grace to endure them and even rejoice in them. The apostle Paul requested God's deliverance from an opportunity/problem he faced, and God said "no," but He gave Paul the grace to handle it with thanksgiving, praise, and even pleasure. What a way to defeat the negative attitude the devil is tempting us with.

> *2 Corinthians 12:8-10*—For this thing I besought the Lord thrice, that it might depart from me. And he said unto me, My grace is sufficient for thee: for my strength is made perfect in weakness. Most gladly therefore will I rather glory in my infirmities, that the power of Christ may rest upon me. Therefore I take pleasure in infirmities, in reproaches, in necessities, in persecutions, in distresses for Christ's sake: for when I am weak, then am I strong.

Negative thinking patterns are rooted in self-love and selfishness. This flies in the face of modern psychology's key principle, "Love yourself first." Lack of self-esteem is not the problem; the difficulty we face in loving God first, then others, is our real struggle. Pride was Satan's original sin and selfishness is at the heart of what the Scripture calls the "pride of life," and as such, it will always be a major struggle for Christians as we go about our lives in an evil, sinful world.

> *Matthew 22:37-40*—Jesus said unto him, Thou shalt love the Lord thy God with all thy heart, and with all thy soul, and with all thy mind. This is the first and great commandment. And the second *is* like unto it, Thou shalt love thy neighbor as thyself. On these two commandments hang all the law and the prophets.

Our children live according to their attitudes, and they pick up their attitudes from our attitudes, which are displayed through our words and actions. If we believe our children ought to act a certain way or have a certain attitude, we must exemplify that behavior in our basic lifestyle choices and mind-set. One of the challenges of this detour is that it is not a ninety-degree departure from the right road. Often this detour appears to be a slight "Y" in the road, a detour so close to the right road that we can reach over and touch it. After a while we can see it in the distance, and then we realize that this slight deviation from the truth has led us to a distant location far from our original intent. This detour is no less dangerous for its benign appearance, because underneath the surface is a cancer that eats away at our children's trust in God.

Companion Scripture Passages:
Romans 8:6, 31-39—Peace from knowing God's love.
1 Samuel 17—I can do what I need to do for God, even if it is hard.
Romans 5:1-5; James 1:2-4—Peace through justification and seeing God's hand in tribulation.

Philippians 2—Four examples of putting others first.
1 Timothy 6:6-21—Admonition on learning contentment.
2 Timothy 2:22; 1 Thessalonians 5:23; 2 Thessalonians 3:16—
Peace.
Ecclesiastes 2:17-23—The final end to a life of hard work without God's will, despair.

Discussions and Study Questions:

1. Despair will come, even when we are doing good things. When we fail to think biblically, what is the result?

2. Which of the self-isms listed do you think is a major problem in today's society? in your family?

3. How can self-protection become a sin?

4. How can love be one of the solutions to this detour?

5. How can faith be one of the solutions to this detour?

6. Which of the seven positive attitudes is your greatest strength?

7. Which of the seven negative attitudes is your greatest weakness?

8. How will you use that awareness in teaching and training your children?

9

DETOUR

NINE

*And, ye fathers, provoke not your children to
wrath: but bring them up in the nurture
and admonition of the Lord.*
Ephesians 6:4

Deprived Discipline

And, ye fathers, provoke not your children to wrath:
but bring them up in the nurture and admonition of the Lord.
Ephesians 6:4

We've all heard the old saying, "A journey of a thousand miles begins with one step." The same is true with the "bringing up" of a godly son or daughter. The twenty or so year journey of rearing that child begins with the first step, that of disciplining his will to submit to authority. Failure to discipline properly in the first few years may be the easy way out for some parents, but in the end, that "easy way" will result in pain and suffering for the parents and in a hard, cruel, and shortened life for their children. I know the process seems backwards, but the fact remains that giving children all they want when they want it is a sure formula for creating major difficulties for them. When we try to make life easier for our children by depriving them of timely discipline and allowing them to get away with selfishness, dishonesty, disrespect, destruction, and disobedience; we are, in fact, making life harder for them and setting the stage for their eventual hurt and heartache.

Let me share with you some Bible verses that prove this backwards principle is absolutely true, making it a dangerous detour to follow.

***Hebrews 12:11*—Now no chastening for the present seemeth to be joyous, but grievous: nevertheless**

**afterward it yieldeth the peaceable fruit of righteous-
ness unto them which are exercised thereby.**

Chastening is an old English word that basically means "discipline." This verse warns us about an illusion concerning the
value and importance of discipline. At first, when discipline is
needed, it would appear, both to the parent and the child, that
the best thing to do is to downplay the need for immediate
disciplinary action. The parent may doubt the child's ability
to understand the command and feel unsure about disciplining for something the child cannot perform. Children are
much smarter than we give them credit for, but we should
be careful of unrealistic expectations.

The wise parent will give commands carefully, assessing the
child's ability for that task before making the command.
When a command is made within the child's ability, the
parent must react properly to any disobedience. The child,
of course, does not want the unpleasantness of being disciplined, and for the parents, the saying, "This hurts me more
than you," may very well be the truth. Therefore, both parties may do anything they can to choose the more seemingly
"joyous" solution and eliminate the discipline. Unfortunately,
that elimination involves ignoring a problem, covering it
up, blame-shifting, or accepting lame excuses. That which
seemed joyous becomes *grievous*; a word that means "painful, sorrowful, causing pain, or experiencing sorrow." How
much better would it be to have the peaceful fruit of righteousness growing in our family than the grievous fruit of
undisciplined children. The earlier we begin discipline, the
easier it is. Remember the old saying, "Pay me now, or pay
me later," reminding us that putting off the unpleasantness
now will not eliminate it but just postpone it!

Proverbs 13:24—He that spareth his rod hateth his son: but he that loveth him chasteneth him betimes.

The word *betimes* was a common word in previous generations and it means "early or to seek early" and carries the implication of "at dawn or very beginning of things." There is no doubt that the Scriptures are admonishing us to begin the discipline process at the very dawn of our children's lives. Such early discipline is an evidence of our love, but a parent who will not discipline early, according to the passage, actually "hates" his son, a word which indicates the depth to which a parent sinks when he ignores this issue in order to indulge in his or her selfishness. It is a terrible thing when, in order to avoid the physical work, the discomfort, the mental attention, and the anguish necessary to properly discipline their young children, parents condone inappropriate behavior with a whole host of excuses and reasons why "it will be better to wait…or at least, in our special case, it will be better." Billy Sunday said, "An excuse is the skin of a reason stuffed with a lie."

Proverbs 19:18—Chasten thy son while there is hope, and let not thy soul spare for his crying.

The phrase *while there is hope* indicates that the time will come when such discipline will do little, if any, good for that child. Clearly, delay in discipline is a very dangerous detour indeed. Why would anyone risk so much for so little? The unpleasantness of a little crying will never outweigh the unpleasantness of the heartache found at the end of this detour.

Proverbs 23:13-14—Withhold not correction from the child: for if thou beatest him with the rod, he shall not die. Thou shalt beat him with the rod, and shalt deliver his soul from hell.

For parents who are believers, the thought of their children refusing to accept Jesus Christ as Savior is indeed frightening. Parents can do many things to "set the stage" for the conversion of their children. They can pray earnestly and diligently; they can regularly expose their children to the Gospel and other Bible stories through consistent attendance at church; they can participate in evangelistic outreaches like Vacation Bible School, Neighborhood Bible Time, and Christian camps; they can teach their children the Bible in daily family devotion times; and they can endorse the truth of their teaching by their personal testimony. Another critical key is early, consistent discipline.

The verses above address the fact that this is the key that may unlock the door to a child's heart, leading to his faith and belief in the Lord Jesus Christ. Some may ask the question as to how discipline can be such a key. First, this discipline must be motivated by love as Jesus Christ spoke of His own love in *Revelation 3:19*, "As many as I love, I rebuke and chasten: be zealous therefore, and repent." No doubt chastening is a tool the Lord uses to bring sinners to repentance, but it is a chastisement that is motivated by love. Second, this kind of discipline must have a goal beyond punishment for some immediate misdeed. A wise parent will be able to connect what is happening in the present to how this incident may very well affect his child's future. In other words, this is discipline with "eternity's values in view." This is a parent not only loving this child, but also loving this child's future.

Now, how does a spanking affect eternity? A phrase by phrase study of *Proverbs 23:13* answers the question.

Withhold not correction from the child

The Hebrew word for *child* is referring to a pre-adolescent child from infancy through puberty. The parent is commanded to make sure that correction (mostly oral instruction on how best to do something) is not withheld (kept away) from the child.

For if thou beatest him with a rod

A study on the word *beatest* reveals that this word refers to striking or hitting lightly and the context would require it to be a non-lethal force. The rod is primarily some type of neutral object, such as a switch or stick. This phrase following the first implies that even if children are lovingly given full and complete instructions as parents are instructed to do, some discipline will be needed so that they may learn the lesson taught. In *2 Timothy 3:16-17* the Lord gives us this same order of personal growth and change. The "profitable" Scriptures first teach us (doctrine) and then reprove us (reproof), showing us what we are doing wrong. Correction is given, educating us on how to do it right. The fourth step of instruction (discipline) shows us the way to habitually live righteously. The end result of teaching, reproving, correcting, and disciplining is found in verse 17, a "*man of God . . . throughly furnished unto all good works.*"

He shall not die

The word translated *die* refers to being killed or dying a premature death. Concerning this verse *The Pulpit Commentary* says, "Do not be weak, thinking that you will injure your child by judicious correction . . . but punish him firmly when necessary . . . ."[1] Children have a way of making a properly administered spanking sound like it is torture unto death. They often make such sounds in order to manipulate parents to cease or put off the dicipline. We must be wise, love their eternal souls, and lovingly discipline them as needed.

And thou shalt deliver his soul from hell

The word *soul* indicates all that is special with this individual life: his will, his emotions, and his intelligence. Hell is *sheol*, the abode of everlasting torment and definitely a place we would want to deliver our children from. Through correction and discipline, parents do their part to deliver or "snatch away" their children from this awful place.

Parents cannot be saved for their children or do anything as an act of grace (such as infant baptism) that will insure their salvation. Each man, woman, boy, or girl must deal personally with God about his or her own sin. Salvation through faith and forgiveness of sins can only be effectual when handled between God and that individual. So this verse is not teaching discipline as a means of grace. It is teaching the principle that a properly disciplined child will be more likely to accept Jesus Christ as his Savior.

Other passages of Scripture that support the value of discipline in the salvation of our children are *Romans 1:5, 6:17,* and *16:26,* which speak of salvation as being "obedience to the faith"; "obeyed from the heart"; and "the obedience of faith." An element of salvation, "by grace . . . through faith" (*Ephesians 2:8*), is tied to a person hearing the gospel, yielding to it in belief, and thus accepting or receiving Jesus Christ. Children who grow up rebelling against authority and disobeying Mom and Dad without any consequences find it much easier to resist "the obedience of faith" and refuse to believe in their hearts on the Lord Jesus Christ.

They know nothing about consequences for disobedience; therefore, hell seems unreal to them. They cannot conceive of a God of love chastening believers now and also punishing unbelievers for eternity. They have said "no" for their entire life and have been allowed to do things their own way. Why not now? Why not for their entire lives? They have received no evidence that the devil's lies are indeed false.

Proverbs 22:6—Train up a child in the way he should go: and when he is old, he will not depart from it.

This passage teaches that children need training as well as correction and that such training will affect the rest of their lives. *Discipline* is often only negatively defined as "punishment." Yet when our Heavenly Father disciplines us, He is not punishing us for our sins. His purpose is to correct us and train us to be more like His Son. When a coach is training a young team of potential athletes, his practices will involve some form of imposed discipline. If one of those athletes is to excel, sooner or later that coach-imposed discipline must be transformed into self-discipline. The degree to which discipline is accepted and implemented will, to a large extent, determine the success of the athlete. Good training, the kind that starts where someone is today and ends with the full realization of that individual's potential, will often go through a seven-step cycle of training.

Cycle of Training

Step 1: Verbal instruction—"say it"
   Give verbal instruction with the clear expectation

Step 2: Practical instruction—"show it"
Illustrate it, do it yourself first, give a visual representation of the verbal instruction

Step 3: Personal practice—"do it"
Encourage them to actually try

Step 4: Positive feedback—"praise it"
Find something in the effort to praise

Step 5: Feedback for improvement—"correct it"
Instruct on how to—this is not saying "you did it wrong"; it is saying "this is how to do it right" This is often just adjustments and fine tuning.

Step 6: Verbal praise and encouragement—"do it again"
Try again with the improvement just learned

Step 7: Challenge to step up to the next level—"what next"
Keep working at improvement

This cycle includes a three step approach to verbal praise: positive words, corrective words, and then follow-up with positive words. Children are better able to handle negative remarks and correction when they are accompanied by words of positive affirmation, value, and love. They must *know* that we love them.

Sometimes people just figure they will deal with problems later hoping things will improve on their own, but they don't. The problem with "Pay me now, or pay me later" is that the "later" price often gets so high that the parties involved are unwilling to pay such a large amount all at once. I remember hearing a particular advertising slogan that said to change the oil and filters when regular maintenance was due on a car, or in the end, put in a new engine. I don't know about you, but I can remember junking two or three vehicles in my past when I was told what a new engine would cost. The cars weren't worth the price. I wonder how many young adults are roaming around today, rebelling against God and living selfishly because, *instead* of paying the price incrementally as the child grew up from infancy, instead the parents deprived their children of the timely discipline they needed. The parents deferred making any payments in "discipline" until, like I did with a car needing a new engine, they said the price was too high. They just threw up their hands and say, "What's the use, the price is too high and he never does what I say anyway!"

On the other hand, parents who begin early to lovingly and consistently discipline children will find that some tune ups are occasionally needed, but most of the major effort required will occur long before the children go through puberty. The total price paid is much less than the cost of depriving our children of this crucial parental responsibility.

[1]Spence, H.O.M., and Exell, Joseph S. *The Pulpit Commentary, Volume 9.* Grand Rapids, Michigan: Wm. B. Eerdmans Publishing Company, 1950, page 442.

Companion Scripture Passages:

1 Samuel 2:22 – 3:21—Contrast the discipline and obedience of Samuel and the discipline and obedience of Eli's sons.

Psalm 78:1-8—What role do the parents play in the choices that their children make?

Proverbs 1-7—These seven chapters outline the value children receive when they listen to and obey their parents.

Ephesians 6:1-4—The key New Testament passage for both parents and children.

Discussion and Study Questions:

1. What does *betimes* mean?

2. What does *chastisement* mean?

3. Discuss "pay me now, or pay me later" in relation to bringing up our children in the nurture (discipline) and admonition (teaching) of the Lord.

4. Which of the seven steps of the training cycle would you have the most trouble with? Why?

5. What is the sandwich approach to verbal feedback?

10

DETOUR

TEN

Fathers, provoke not your children to anger,
lest they be discouraged.
Colossians 3:21

Discouraging Dads

*Fathers, provoke not your children to anger,
lest they be discouraged.*
Colossians 3:21

The word *discouraged* in *Colossians 3:21* occurs only once in the Scriptures and *Strong's* defines it as "disheartened, dispirited, broken in spirit." *Vine's* adds to that definition "negative spirit... denoting feeling, passion; hence Eng., fume."[1] By investigating further, we can discover the *Webster's 1828 Dictionary* definition of *fume*: "To be in a rage; to be hot with anger. He frets, he fumes, he stares, he stamps the ground." Anger sounds like a very detrimental detour for our children.

Ephesians 6:4 says, "And, ye fathers, provoke not your children to wrath: but bring them up in the nurture and admonition of the Lord." *Vine's* definition of *provoke* means "to arouse to wrath,"[2] and by using *wrath* instead of *anger,* the Holy Spirit indicates a "more agitated condition of the feelings, an outburst of wrath from inward indignation...wrath expresses more the inward feeling...It is characteristic (of wrath) that it quickly blazes up and quickly subsides, though that is not necessarily implied in each case."[3]

This detour often leads to discouraged, disheartened children because Dads, in their special office of "Father," can and often do ignite this inner fire of anger within their children. The Scripture indicates that fathers bear the primary responsibility in these two passages, but the context of the verses and the testimony of all of Scripture is that both parents share the responsibility to "train up a child in the way he should go" (*Proverbs 22:6*). Undoubtedly, one of the chief characteristics of today's generation is a deep-seated, seething anger that erupts periodically as aggressive, verbal abuse, often leading to physical violence. At other times, anger turns inward, becoming self-destructive. In whatever way anger manifests itself, the detoured road of the angry man's future leads far away from the straight, narrow path God desires for our children.

Anger can be exhibited outwardly as stubbornness, impatience, frustration, sullenness, resentment, or depression. Anger is verbalized by whining, complaining, using sarcastic, mean, or critical words, or by aggressive arguing.

The Biblical Counseling Series, indicates there are three principle causes of anger:[4]

1. Frustration produced by a thwarted goal, disappointment, interrupted plans, or some type of continued aggravation
2. Displeasure at having to endure hurt from people or circumstances
3. Fear brought on by a variety of things—some type of loss, insecurity, or inability to control a situation

Each of these three causes can be traced to the twin sins of pride and selfishness, and when counseling angry children or adults, we must consider these two root sins. There are a number of good resource tools for parents who want to study this detour in more depth, tools that not only give references and principles from God's Word, but also provide step-by-step, practical suggestions for dealing with anger in the home.

The emphasis of our discussion concerning this dangerous detour is that the way we discipline (nurture), teach (admonish), and train our children can, in itself, be what diverts our children into this dead-end detour. We must learn how to nurture biblically through discipline, how to admonish through our example and words, and how to train our children in a way that not only honors them, but also enables them to honor their parents and other authorities. Ignoring the danger of anger and disregarding the possible provocations to anger for our children is, at the very least, disobedient to God's commands in the verses above and could divert our children to a path that leads to destruction. This detour is going nowhere productive.

Sequential Stages of Upbringing

The scriptural idea of training up our children taught in *Proverbs 22:6* indicates that there is a process that begins when they are young. When a child is first born, he is completely dependent on Mom and Dad for survival, and our goal for 18 to 22 years later is to have that same child ready to become completely independent of Mom and Dad, able to earn a living, make wise decisions, rear his own children, and continue in his own personal spiritual growth. If we don't want to provoke our children to wrath, we must rear them sequentially. When we get these steps out of order, the mix-up naturally creates a climate of anger in the hearts of our children.

There are four stages or sequences of bringing up children:

1. **Discipline or Control Stage**
    We are training children to submit to our authority when we have complete control over almost every aspect of their lives. This sets the stage for correct relationships to all other authority in their lives.

2. **Training Stage**—*when we teach the "what" of life*
   We are training children in character development habits
   and in the basic facts and knowledge of life. They will know
   over 50% of everything they will ever learn before they leave
   this pre-puberty stage. Our control over them at this stage
   is lessened considerably, primarily because they have grown
   up a little and have started doing things for themselves. But
   parents should still primarily be in control of their lives.

3. **Teaching Stage**—*when we teach the "why" of life*
   During this post-puberty to young adult stage, we are training our teens by constantly teaching and answering "why"
   questions. Seemingly, parental control is lessening almost
   daily. As they are able to assume greater responsibilities, we
   are more comfortable with their growing independence.
   They drive the car and often go places and do things without
   us. The parent's goal during this time is to enlarge the teen's
   freedom by degrees as the young person demonstrates he
   has matured enough to take the next step.

4. **Advice and Counsel Stage**
   Our children are now old enough to be legally out on their
   own, and some of them are. The time for telling them exactly
   what to do next is past, and we are really pleased if, as fruit
   of our nurturing, they are seeking us out for advice. A wise
   parent will answer most questions with other questions that
   go back to biblical and foundational principles upon which
   we hope our children will build their lives.

There is actually a fifth stage, the **Love Stage**. It is not listed as
a separate time in their lives because they must experience our
unconditional love for them at all times and in all stages. Our
love may be demonstrated in different ways at different stages
of their lives, but it must be constantly demonstrated.

Now the problem begins when parents switch the proper sequence of the stages, thereby building into their children's lives a deep, burning anger in the process. These parents allow very young children to do what they please, doing almost nothing to control their impulses. Parents often choose to control the environment rather than to discipline the young child. They "child-proof" a home rather than take the time and effort to teach and discipline the children to control their impulses. Then, when the children are older and begin doing things that could severely damage their health or ruin their lives, parents, because of fear, clamp down with controls at the very time children should be given more freedom. The parents have switched the sequences of the complete control stage and the expanding freedom stages and such a reversal makes young people begin to fume!

Feared Family Breakup

Another key way that parents provoke their children to anger is by bringing them up in an atmosphere charged with FEAR! Something new has exploded in America in the last two generations. In a recently published book entitled *The Bridger Generation*[5], the author identifies fear of family break-up and fear of having an unstable family of their own as the major fears of today's generation of young people. These fears are major causes or roots of anger in people, especially because they are tied to the loss of something every person holds very dear to himself, a stable loving home with both Mom and Dad. Divorce is actually harder on children than the death of a parent. When Mom and Dad cannot get along in the home and the children doubt their relationship even a little, parents are creating an atmosphere that scares their children to ANGER! Having a loving relationship with our spouse without arguing, bickering, or fighting, is the best thing we can do for our children.

I once surveyed a group of young teens that I was teaching, asking them what their parents did that made them angry. The results follow in no particular order, but just as I tallied them. I found really interesting that all but five of them (numbers *1, 3, 16, 17,* and *20*) deal with the confusion of switching the control and freedom stages of upbringing. Can you see how the others are all related to this problem? Here are their responses:

Ways Parents Provoke Teens to Wrath
1. Being inconsistent
2. Not letting you do what you want
3. Being a hypocrite
4. Closed mind
5. No trust
6. Don't let you grow up
7. Don't believe in you—no independence
8. You're expected to respect them and they don't respect you
9. They won't let you give your side of the story
10. Always telling you something—on your case, but you don't know why
11. What you've done is never good enough
12. Bring up past to load issue
13. Tell you three times in a row—nagging
14. Ignore you when you're trying to talk
15. Make fun of me or discipline me in public
16. Play favorites
17. Parents kiss in public
18. Want you to be over-achiever or super student
19. Serve parents hand and foot and not do anything for them
20. Don't spend time with you and listen
21. Use your dependence as a club
22. You want to be alone and they won't let you

Contrasting Love and Anger

Love is the basic characteristic of all of a Christian's relationships in life. *Galatians 5:14-15* says we should love our neighbor as ourselves, and the consequences of not doing so is that we will "bite [thwart, vex, irritate] and devour [consume or destroy one another] one another."[6]

> *Galatians 5:14-15*—For all the law is fulfilled in one word, *even* in this; thou shalt love thy neighbor as thyself. But if ye bite and devour one another, take heed that ye be not consumed one of another.

The obvious application of these verses to our home (members of our family are definitely our neighbors) is that without love in the home we will be feeding on and destroying the other members of our family. In the verses following, we find that the works of the flesh produce, among other things, hatred, strife, and wrath (*Galatians 5:20*), while the fruit of the Spirit produces the qualities of love, peace, and longsuffering, which is patience with people (*Galatians 5:22*). The implication is that if we follow the impulses of our sinful flesh, the easy, selfish way, we will produce many attitudes, including wrath, that will destroy those closest to us (*Proverbs 22:24-25*). On the other hand, if we allow the Holy Spirit to freely work within us, He will produce the self-sacrificial love that is characteristic of Christ's love for us.

Since love should characterize our family's relationships and since parental anger is a major cause of children's wrath, we need to see clearly the ways love and anger contradict each other. When parents do not show the same patience (an attribute of love) to their own children that they show to others, children will mirror the explosive, unpredictable, and loud responses of their parents.

Which of these "ways" characterizes your parent/child relationship?

God's Way—Love
Love is patient; is kind; not easily provoked (*1 Corinthians 13:4,5*).
Man's Way—Anger
There is no patience with children in the home; the least little thing sets the parent "off." Anger explodes in a rage or temper, striking out physically or verbally at people or things, or seethes inwardly and becoming bitter.

God's Way—Love
Love is not arrogant; "not puffed up" (*1 Corinthians 13:4*).
Man's Way—Anger
Anger characterizes itself as "righteous indignation" or "justifiable" instead of accepting responsibility for one's actions and asking for forgiveness (disregarding *Matthew 7:1-5; Ephesians 4:31; Hebrews 12:15; James 1:19-25; 3:13-4:2*).

God's Way—Love
Love does not act unbecomingly (*1 Corinthians 13:5*).
Man's Way—Anger
Anger "loses it temper" by name calling, publically embarassing a child, throwing objects, yelling at others, etc.

God's Way—Love
Love endures all things (*1 Corinthians 13:7*).
Man's Way—Anger
Anger demonstrates a lack of trust in God's sovereignty. Rather than viewing difficult disciplining times as God-appointed opportunities to teach, the child is made to feel he is a burden and not of value.

God's Way—Love
Love vaunteth not itself, is not puffed up (*1 Corinthians 13:4*).
Man's Way—Anger
Anger is rooted in pride and is intolerant of anything that interferes with "me."

Anger is listed with many other vile and hurtful sins (*Colossians 3:8 and Ephesians 4:31*), and is considered a work of the flesh (*Galatians 5:19*); however Scripture allows anger when it is used properly as emotional energy to deal righteously with the problems and challenges we are facing. Kittle says, "*Ephesians 4:26* allows that even believers might be angry at times, but if they are, they must be careful not to sin. *James 1:19* teaches a forbearance that, like God's, is more ready to forgive than to yield to anger, for anger does not advance true righteousness."[7]

> *Ephesians 4:26-27*—Be ye angry, and sin not: let not the sun go down upon your wrath: neither give place to the devil.

When we provoke our children to wrath, we expose them to a variety of Satan's attacks. The Greek word used in *Ephesians 4:26* refers to a marked-off place, especially, a place marked off as a staging area used by the military as a base of operations when invading a foreign country. Metaphorically, it means an opportunity or occasion for acting. The application seems clear enough that to give place to the devil is to give him an occasion to attack and a base of operations from which he can launch his attacks. There is no telling how the devil will use this foothold once he has gained it in our children's hearts.

Further Dangers of Anger

Anger has far reaching consequences beyond the immediate manifestation of that anger.

1. Anger leads to revenge that, in essence, usurps God's divine prerogative of judgment *(Romans 12:19)*.

2. Anger may lead to God's chastisement as our anger may lead to His response of wrath *(Colossians 3:6-8)*.

3. Anger seems to be contagious to others, especially our children *(Colossians 3:8; Ephesians 6:4)*.

4. Anger may affect our prayer life *(1 Timothy 2:8)*.

5. Anger may disqualify our children from future Christian service *(Titus 1:7)*.

6. Anger may lead to sin if not handled properly *(Ephesians 4:26)*.

7. Anger escalates to other relationship sins *(Ephesians 4:31; Proverbs 29:22)*.

8. Anger destroys communication *(Proverbs 18:19)*.

9. Anger destroys one's reputation as it leads others to consider the quick-to-anger person a fool *(Proverbs 12:16; 14:29)*.

10. Anger can lead a child into a life of cruelty to others, even to those who should be most loved *(Proverbs 27:3-4; Genesis 49:7)*.

Anger is not only expressed by outward expressions of temper, but also displayed by:

- Unreasonable demands
- Distortion of the truth, exaggerations, half-truths, slander, and lies
- Displeasure at little or no provocation
- Destruction of property, animals, work in progress, relationships, or any tangible or intangible items of value
- Repression, silence, and withdrawal
- Critical, cruel, evil words
- Seeking sympathy and alliances with third parties, who can do nothing to help the situation
- An argumentative and contentious spirit

- A slow, seething burn, not apparent for years to come
- Bitterness that will defile many, if left unchecked

So, how can we bring up a child to maturity without provoking him to wrath? We will answer that question with three thoughts:

1. **Provide a balance in our discipline and training that is both age-appropriate and biblically sound as illustrated below.**

   Bring Up
   To nourish to maturity, not just physically, but in all areas of life. This is a process that starts at birth and continues until the child leaves the home. Proper sequences are essential. *Ephesians 6:4*—And, ye fathers, provoke not your children to wrath: but bring them up in the nurture and admonition of the Lord.

   Nurture—Training
   Paideia—The whole training and education of children as it relates to the cultivation of the mind and morals using commands, teaching, reproofs, and punishment. Following up verbal instruction by showing how and being a good example are essential.

   Admonition—Teaching
   Training that is done primarily, but not exclusively by word. It includes exhortation, encouragement, teaching, remonstrance, reproof, or blame as required. It is an appeal to the intellect and reason, but it may involve correction by deed if necessary.

2. Know our children; know what they need and don't need at each stage of the maturing process.

What do they like? What is their personality style? What are their strengths and weaknesses? What is their spiritual condition? Are they saved, for sure? Who are their friends? What irritates them? In what character areas do they need to grow? At what responsibility level are they? What temptations do they seem to have the most trouble with? The better we know them, the better we will relate and respond to them. Once we know them, we can tailor our discipline and teaching to fit them and their situation. As an example, I am including a general list of what the average teen is crying out for as he tries to grow up.

The Needs of Young Adults (Post-Puberty Children)

- To have their doubts settled and believe in absolute truth.
- To have a feeling of movement toward independence. Set up some sequences that will give them a sense of progress.
- To be understood in the growing importance of friendships. Teach them, what is a "friend?"
- To practice reasoning and abstract thinking skills. Ask many questions.

- To expand their interests and horizons. Camp is a great place for this.
- To give and receive respect.
- To practice sacrificial "others-first" type of loving service, at church, or family "missions" projects.
- To make wise life decisions and learn to solve problems.
- To develop personal Bible-based standards and convictions.
- To learn to react to people and circumstances properly.
- To learn and practice biblical relationship skills.
- To accept and fulfill responsibility and accountability.
- To learn to be trustworthy.

3. **Finally, as parents, we must work within our family not to provoke our children to wrath.**
    Sometimes parents want a specific list of do's and don'ts regarding provoking their children to anger, but the subject goes much deeper than that. The following list should "prime the pump" and get our mind going in figuring out how to do this business of "bringing them up" in a wise and biblical manner without provoking them to anger.

Parents of Young Adults Need to ...
- Spend more time with them (work on finding some "common ground").
- Show unconditional love.
- Loosen control with fulfilled responsibilities.
- Love your spouse and be a biblical role example.
- Know, teach, and reason the "why" of rules and beliefs.
- Set and be consistent with reasonable boundaries and expectations.

- Be good examples of what you teach, believe, and value.
- Be faithful in prayer for your children.
- Be unshockable, listening, question-asking advisors.
- Establish some guidance in the area of dating and courtship.
- Help them develop a biblical and eternal "world view."

Parents of Young Adults Beware of . . .
- Too tight in control (reverse of creation order) as they get close to independence.
- Inappropriate punishment that does not match the offense.
- Public criticism (viewed as being disloyal).
- Refusal to discuss and reason through a question or disagreement.
- Constant nagging and being too pushy.
- Failure to properly model what is expected of them.
- Attempt to isolate them from all outside influences.
- Inconsistency in application of rules and consequences.

The detour of discouraging Dads who provoke their children to anger is one of the more subtle, destructive, and long lasting detours off the road of life. The Scripture indicates that the result of such provocation to anger will result in our children turning off onto the detour of discouragement, which means to lose spirit or heart or to become sullen.

Colossians 3:21—Fathers, provoke not your children *to anger,* lest they be discouraged.

The long-range effects of sinful anger will be an inflated view of self, a distorted view of others, and a diluted view of God.

This will, in turn, lead to a life of shattered relations without the blessing that God sends those who honor and obey Him and His Word. We want to keep our children from even considering this detour as a way of life, because anger almost guarantees failure in the areas of life that are most important and of eternal value.

In order to deter our children from taking this detour, we must make sure we are bringing them up in the proper sequences, without the fear of a family breakup, and in a true atmosphere of love. We are then on the right road to eliminating the dangers that anger brings to a family. Then, on the positive side, we must bring them up in an atmosphere of balanced discipline with admonition (teaching), coupled with both a clear knowledge of each child and a desire to work at the practical aspects of doing the right things at the right time. Being forewarned of this dangerous detour, we should be forearmed. We can do much in our Christian homes to keep from raising angry children, and as we do, the blessings of obedience will come in their lives.

[1]Vine, W. E. *Vine's Expository Dictionary of Old and New Testament Words.* Old Tappan, New Jersey: Fleming H. Revell Company, 1981, page 316.

[2]Ibid., page 228.

[3]Ibid., pages 56-57.

[4]Berg, Jim. *Introduction to Biblical Counseling.* Greenville, South Carolina: Bob Jones University, 1992, page 23.

[5]Rainer, Thom S. *Bridger Generation*. Nashville: Broadman and Holman Publishers, 1997, page 119.

[6]Zodhiates, Spiros. *Complete Word Study Dictionary.* Chattanooga, Tennessee: AMG Publishers, 1992, pages 396 and 849.

[7]Kittel, Gerhard, and Friedrich, Gerhard, Editors. *The Theological Dictionary of the New Testament, Abridged in One Volume.* Grand Rapids, Michigan: William B. Eerdman's Publishing Company, 1985, *anger / wrath (orgeu).*

Companion Scripture Passages:
Leviticus 19:17-18
Ephesians 2:3; 6:4; 4:26-27
Proverbs 16:32; 25:28; 15:1
James 1:19-22
Colossians 3:8
James 3:13-18
Psalms 37:8

Discussion and Study Questions:

1. What are the three major causes for sinful anger?

2. Why is some anger permissible?

3. How can we as parents be setting the stage for having an angry teenager by not disciplining them properly when they are toddlers?

4. What are some ways you may have been provoking your children to wrath that you could avoid by making some changes? Ask yourself these questions:

   a. What am I currently doing?

   b. How does that unnecessarily encourage inappropriate anger?

   c. What will I do differently?

5. What are some appropriate ways to properly balance discipline and admonition?

DETOUR APPENDIX

DANGEROUS DETOURS

	The Detour	Deals With	Destination
1.	Delayed Discernment	Teaching	No Personal Convictions Formed *Hebrews 4:12-14*
2.	Defiling Bitterness	Forgiveness	Torment of Self *Matthew 18:34-35* Defile Others *Hebrews 12:15*
3.	Dishonorable Deportment	Respect	Poor Quality of Life Shortened Quantity of Life *Ephesians 6:1-3*
4.	Disobeying Duties	Authority	Rebellious; Unruly *1 Timothy 3:4-5*
5.	Disbelieving Practices	Example	Reject Teaching *Philippians 4:9* *2 Thessalonians 3:9*
6.	Dominating Discontentment	Goals	Covetousness and Greed *Hebrews 13:5*
7.	Distracted Parents	Priorities	Time Spent Foolishly Children feel unloved without time *Ephesians 5:15-17*
8.	Deliberate Despair	Thinking Patterns	Negative Thinking Worry; Fear; No Peace *Philippians 4:6-8*
9.	Deprived Discipline	The Will	No Submission Possibly No Salvation *Romans 10:13*
10.	Discouraging Dads	Anger	Give Place to Devil, Thus Allowing Dangerous Temptations *Ephesians 6:10-12; 4:26-27*

LEARNING CONTENTMENT

1 Timothy 6:6-19

In order to learn to be content, we must use the 3F Formula

1. **F_____—"to move away from; to seek safety by flight"** *(v.11)*

   a. We must not have a _____ goal based on materialism (*Matthew 6:33*).

   b. We must not _____ money. Greed is the belief that money is _____and can give me _____.

2. **F_____ —"to press toward the mark; not a casual attitude"** *(v.11)*

   a. Righteousness—right living as a child of God.

   b. Godliness—pursuing a godly lifestyle with Christ as our example.

   c. Faith—belief in the unseen things talked of in the Bible so that one acts on their reality.

   d. Love—self-sacrificing desire to meet the needs of the loved one.

   e. Patience—steadfastness; not swerving from one's purpose; endurance.

   f. Meekness—accepting all God's dealing with us as good.

3. **F_____—"to persistently resist opposition and temptation; to labor or fervently strive for"** *(v.12-19)*

   a. Fight the good fight of _____through

      1) Establishing an _____value system.

    2)   _____the God in Whom we
        place our faith.
        a)   God Who _____all-omniscient
        b)   God Who gives_____-creator;
            the highest creative act of God-to give life
        c)   God Who reveals Himself through_____
            __ _____by His Word-incarnation;
            sinless life; death and burial; resurrection;
            ascension and return; intercession
        d)   God Who_____the universe
        e)   God Who is _____(eternal)
            and controls_____as His own
        f)   God Who is to be_____
        g)   God Who has_____power
            and might

  b.   Charge (to give responsibility with firmness)   believers with material possessions to live by faith.
     1)   Live by faith through their_____
         •   Humility
         •   Trust
         •   Gratitude
     2)   Live by faith through their_____
         •   Kindness
         •   Generosity
         •   Preparation

STUDY THE WORD

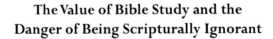

The Value of Bible Study and the
Danger of Being Scripturally Ignorant

1. Ignorance is a tool of the _____.

    2 Corinthians 4:4—In whom the god of this world hath blinded the minds of them which believe not, lest the light of the glorious gospel of Christ, who is the image of God, should shine unto them.

2. Ignorance is a symptom of spiritual _____.

    2 Peter 1:9—But he that lacketh these things is blind, and cannot see afar off, and hath forgotten that he was purged from his old sins.

3. Ignorance is a characteristic of those who cannot _____ with brothers (fellow believers).

    1 John 2:11—But he that hateth his brother is in darkness, and walketh in darkness, and knoweth not whither he goeth, because that darkness hath blinded his eyes.

4. Ignorance is a characteristic of _____ and conceit.

    Romans 11:25—For I would not, brethren, that ye should be ignorant of this mystery, lest ye should be wise in your own conceits; that blindness in part is happened to Israel, until the fullness of the Gentiles be come in.

FOUR LEVELS OF BIBLE STUDY

Level One—Reading for _____ and content—*Proverbs 1:7,22,29; 2:1-9*

> *2 Peter 1:5—And beside this, giving all diligence, add to your faith virtue; and to virtue knowledge.*

Level Two—Reading for devotion and_____
—*Psalm 25:4-12*

> *Job 23:12—Neither have I gone back from the commandment of his lips; I have esteemed the words of his mouth more than my necessary food.*

Level Three—Study for personal spiritual growth and _____ (application)—*Psalm 1; Psalm 19:7-14; Psalm 119:15,23,48,78,97,99,148*

> *Joshua 1:7-8—Only be thou strong and very courageous, that thou mayest observe to do according to all the law, which Moses my servant commanded thee: turn not from it to the right hand or to the left, that thou mayest prosper whithersoever thou goest. This book of the law shall not depart out of thy mouth; but thou shalt meditate therein day and night, that thou mayest observe to do according to all that is written therein: for then thou shalt make thy way prosperous, and then thou shalt have good success.*

Level Four—Study for _____and _____—*Hebrews 5:12; 2 Timothy 2:2,24-25; Proverbs 9:9; Deuteronomy 6:1,7; Matthew 28:19; Acts 5:42; 1 Timothy 6:2*

> *Ezra 7:10—For Ezra had prepared his heart to seek the law of the LORD, and to do it, and to teach in Israel statutes and judgments.*

PRACTICAL HELPS FOR CONSISTENT BIBLE STUDY

1. Set up a prayer and Bible reading journal.

2. Volunteer to teach Sunday School, junior church, etc.

3. Get the proper study aids and tools. (Concordance, Topical Bible, Times and Customs helps, Word definition helps, One-volume commentary, Interpretation helps—*Bible Explorers Guide* by J. Phillips)

4. See It Big—Keep It Simple

   a. It is more important than food.

   b. The Word is equated with God, "the word was God."

   c. The highest TIME priority of each day—*Matthew 6:33.*

      Ephesians 5:15-16—See then that ye walk circumspectly, not as fools, but as wise, redeeming the time, because the days are evil.
      - *Circumspectfully*—no waste; save; without interruption
      - *Not as fools*—plan study time. Compare *Hebrews 5:11* and *Proverbs 6:6-11*
      - *Redeem*—to buy back, to get all of a rare item possible. Time-use evaluations are essential.

5. Be honest with what the Scripture actually says.

   a. No more, no less

   b. Don't add to or subtract from

   c. Depart not from the right or to the left

   d. The teacher/ambassador's job is to accurately repeat what the "master" says

DAILY DEVOTIONAL JOURNAL

Date: _____ **Passage Read:** _____

Comments on the passage:_____
_____
_____
_____

My meditation thought or principle for the day:_____
_____
_____
_____

- ☐ Did I work on a memory verse today?
- ☐ Do I remember my meditation thought or principle from yesterday?
- ☐ Did I share yesterday's thought or principle with someone?

Today's praises:_____
_____
_____

Today's intercession:_____
_____
_____

Today's requests:_____
_____
_____

LIFE PRINCIPLES

Record principle here: _____

_____
_____
_____
_____

Based on the Authority of:

List out the verses you used to help you determine this principle. Write out the key proof verse.

Goals for This Principle:

Write a goal for this principle. Goals should be specific, measurable, and attainable.

What This Principle Means on a Daily Basis:

List specific changes that should result in your life in one or more of these role areas.
☐ *Testimony*   ☐ *Church*   ☐ *Family*   ☐ *Occupation*   ☐ *Neighbor*

Accountability Plan:

Record target date on your calendar. Record your progress, difficulties, and struggles.
☐ *Calendar (Personal)*   ☐ *Spouse / Friend*   ☐ *Mentor: Name* _____

God's Organizational Chart of Family Roles

*But I would have you know, that the head of every man is Christ, and
the head of the woman is the man, and the head of Christ is God.*
1 Corinthians 11:3

TEAM	INDIVIDUAL	ROLE

GOD — **FATHER**

TRINITY
Adopted children of God
Romans 8:14-17

CHRIST — **SON**

MAN — **HUSBAND**

PARENTS
FATHER/MOTHER

CHILDREN

WOMAN — **WIFE**

Communicator

With your words—Ephesians 4:29; 1 Thessalonians 2:11
With your ears—listen well, Matthew 13:13-15; Proverbs 15:32-33; 18:13
With controlled communication—Proverbs 11:9, 13, 29
Without self-serving arguing—Philippians 2:3
With proper answers—Proverbs 15:1

Teacher

Become qualified to teach through spiritual growth—Hebrews 5:12-14
Teach your children—Psalms 78:5; Ephesians 6:4; Deuteronomy 6:7
Teach your wife—1 Corinthians 14:35

Prayer Warrior

Of a righteous man—James 5:16
With Christ's example—Luke 6:12
For all things—Philippians 4:6
At meal time—1 Timothy 4:5
With thanksgiving—Philippians 4:6; Luke 6:12

Lover

With sacrificial love—Ephesians 5:22-33
With attitude of love—Colossians 3:19
With physical love—1 Corinthians 7:2-5
With giving love—John 3:16
With God's priorities—Matthew 22:37-40; Luke 14:26

Leader

Qualification for church leadership—1 Timothy 3:4,5,12; Titus 1:6
Effect on followers—Matthew 15:14
Example of Christ's leadership—Ephesians 5:23
Accountability of leaders to God—Hebrews 13:17; James 3:1
Leadership of family—Genesis 18:19

Worker

Providing for the family—1 Timothy 5:8
Being faithful always—1 Corinthians 4:2
Using Christ's example—John 5:17; 9:4; 17:4
Following God's command—Genesis 3:19
Using the principle of "no work - no eat"—2 Thessalonians 3:10,12

Learner

Learn God's Word—1 Peter 2:2; 2 Timothy 2:15
Learn in order to teach children—Deuteronomy 6:6
Learn about your wife—1 Peter 3:7
Learn how to train children—Proverbs 22:6
Learn to lead and manage the home—1 Timothy 3:3-4

Submitter

To each other—Ephesians 5:21
To God—James 4:17
To spiritual authority—Hebrews 13:17
To temporal authority—1 Peter 2:13-15

A LOVING LEADER IS A...

DETOUR

ANSWER KEY

ANSWER KEY

Chapter 1

1a. Recognizing
1b. Teach; explain
2. Doubt; reject
3a. Unable
3b. Unwilling
4. Being saved
5a. Pray consistently for wisdom
5b. Live obediently now
5c. Ask for advice from discerning church leaders and stay consistent in church
5d. Pray for the Holy Spirit's illumination of Scriptures
5e. Study the Scriptures
5f. Continue to grow
7. When parents are unwilling to learn and teach discernment to their children

Chapter 2

2. Self-sacrificing
3. Attitudes, words
4. Attitudes, words
5. Ignorance, self

Chapter 3

1a. Displaying
1b. Lukewarm
1c. Inconsistency
1d. Arguments
1e. Hypocritical
2a. Detective

2b. Wisdom

4. First in list of relational commands (last six commandments) in Ten Commandments

5. Displaying pride

Chapter 4

1a. Given

1b. Earned

2a. Lovingly lead

2b. Headship

3. Voluntary, equal

4. Role, equal, love

8. God

Chapter 5

1. Accumulation

3. Pattern

Chapter 6

1. Exodus 20:17—Thou shalt not covet thy neighbor's
house, thou shalt not covet thy neighbor's wife, nor his
manservant, nor his maidservant, nor his ox, nor his ass,
nor any thing that is thy neighbor's.

2. Idolatry

3. Acting as though God cannot meet our needs and provide
for our necessities and turning to the world to provide
peace and happiess for us

4. Do all things through Christ

5. When the things of the world choke out the Word, materialism will change our goals and the way we live

6. Tells us what to flee from, what to follow, and what to aggressively fight

Chapter 7

2. Confusion from a multiplicity of objects crowding on the mind and calling the attention different ways; perturbation of mind; perplexity; as, the family was in a state of distraction (*Webster's, 1828 Dictionary*).
4. T-I-M-E
5. Because the days are evil (full of labors, annoyances, hardships, and wickedness) and full of peril to our Christian faith and steadfastness
6. To purchase back, to repurchase what has been sold, to redeem time is to use more diligence in the improvement of it; to be diligent and active in duty and preparation
7. Like—can spend it; Unlike—cannot save it

Chapter 8

1. We are exhibiting a lack of faith or a lack of knowledge of God and of His nature and power.
3. When we fail to rely on God for protection and rely on self, we will have increasing fears and anxiety. God commands us not to worry and fret but to cast our cares on Him.
4. When we love and serve God and others above ourselves, we will not teach our children a self-absorbed attitude. The more we focus on ourselves, the easier it is to give in to despair.
5. When we trust God above trusting other people or ourselves, we will not teach our children self-sufficiency. We will teach them God-sufficiency.

Chapter 9

1. Betimes—early or to seek early; at dawn or very beginning of things
2. Chastisement—discipline

5. Positive words, corrective words, follow-up with positive words

Chapter 10

1. (1) Frustration produced by a thwarted goal, disappointment, interrupted plans, or some type of continued aggravation, (2) Displeasure at having to endure hurt from people or circumstances, (3) Fear brought on by a variety of things including some type of loss, insecurity, or inability to control a situation

2. Scripture allows anger when it is used properly as emotional energy to deal righteously with the problems and challenges we are facing. Kittel says, "*Ephesians 4:26* allows that even believers might be angry at times, but if they are, they must be careful not to sin."

3. By parents switching the proper sequence of the stages of discipline or control, training, teaching, and advice and counsel. When a toddler is allowed to do as he pleases, he will continue to want to do as he pleases. When what the teen wants to do will harm him long-term, the parent will often clamp down with control. The control and training should have been in the early years. The clamping down then causes anger in the teen.

Appendix—Study the Word

1. Devil
2. Blindness
3. Walk or get along
4. Pride

Level One—Knowledge
Level Two—Fellowship
Level Three—Meditation

Level Four—Teaching and Application

Learning Contentment

1. Flee
    a. Life
    b. Love, all, all
2. Follow
    a. Righteousness
    b. Godliness
    c. Faith
    d. Love
    e. Patience
    f. Meekness
3. Fight
    a. Faith
        1) Eternal
        2) Knowing
            a) Sees
            b) Life
            c) Jesus Christ
            d) Rules
            e) Immortal, time
            f) Honored
            g) Everlasting
    b. 1) Attitudes
        2) Actions

ABOUT THE AUTHOR

Walt and Betty Brock have been in ministry for over 35 years, working with all ages of children and teens along with parents. After serving several years as a youth pastor and Christian schoolteacher, in 1973 Walt co-founded Ironwood, a western Christian camp in the high desert of southern California, where he continues to serve as Executive Director. Walt continues to be involved in education, serving as administrator of Ironwood Christian Academy that was started in 1980 and serving as CFO for the Golden State Association of Christian Schools. Walt serves on several boards, speaks at family and leadership conferences, as well as other seminar speaking.

The Brocks have four children and ten grandchildren. Two of their children serve at Ironwood with their families: Sam is director of Ironwood and Shannon [Steuerwald] is principal of the school. Daniel teaches in a Christian school, and David is a college pastor. Serving God in the various ministries with their children is one of Walt and Betty's greatest joys.

Reaching the heart of young people for the Lord Jesus Christ, strengthening families, and serving local churches has been Walt's burden over his many years of service. Knowing that parents are the major key to the heart issues of young people, he has written this book as a help for parents in rearing godly children who will desire to serve God. Walt's desire is that all three goals of reaching young people, strengthening families, and serving local churches will be met as a result of reading and applying God's principles of parenting.

Brock Children & Spouses

Daniel, Sam, David & Shannon

Sam & Cindy, David & Tiffany, Walt & Betty,
Daniel & Esther, Steve & Shannon

From top left: Betty, Courtney, Shannon,
Florence (Walt's mom) & Birdie (Betty's mom)

Four Generations

Youngest to oldest: Bodie, Sam, Walt & Lee

WALT'S FAMILY

John & Judy Brock, Walt & Betty Brock at their parent's 60th wedding anniversary celebration in June, 2003.

BROCK GRANDCHILDREN

THE BROCK FAMILY

The Brocks have been known for interesting traditions in their family. When all of them get together, you never know quite what to expect. It would seem that there is never a dull moment especially with 10 grandkids running around, but sometimes the grown adults will be more boisterous and out-going than the kids. All of Walt and Betty's children and their families are involved in ministry, and it is a blessing to see the godly values that are being passed on to the next generation of Brocks. But beware, you never know what to expect when you are with the Brock clan!